Attitude
how to be the coolest girl you know

Tips to Help You
Deal, Feel, and
Be Real

by Lisa McCourt
and Aimee McCourt

illustrations by Treesha Runnells Vaux

LOWELL HOUSE JUVENILE

LOS ANGELES

NTC/Contemporary Publishing Group

*For Lisa—who has taught me so many things about life
and love and who inspires me every day by just being the
wonderful person she is.*
—A.M.

For Aimee—You ROCK, cool girl.
—L.M.

**With lots of love, we want to thank Bettye McCourt and Polly
Hogan, the supercool women in our family who gave us the room
and the inspiration to be our best selves.**

Published by Lowell House
A division of NTC/Contemporary Publishing Group, Inc.
4255 West Touhy Avenue, Lincolnwood (Chicago), Illinois 60712 U.S.A.

Managing Director and Publisher: Jack Artenstein
Director of Publishing Services: Rena Copperman
Editorial Director: Brenda Pope-Ostrow
Project Editor: Amy Downing
Designer: Treesha Runnells Vaux
Cover Model: Stephanie Copperman
Cover Photo: Halstan Williams

Printed and bound in the United States of America

Library of Congress Catalog Card Number: 99-76530

ISBN: 0-7373-0336-0

DHD 10 9 8 7 6 5 4 3 2

What's an ATTITUDE and how can I get one?

Your attitude is more than what you look like, how you spend your time, who you hang with, or what you wear. It tells people who you are more than any other thing about you. The one you choose for yourself has the power to make or break the rest of your school years. And what's so cool is that no matter what's going on in your life, your attitude is the one thing that YOU have complete control over. YOU get to pick it; you get to change it; you're the one who lives with it. This book is full of ideas and tips about all kinds of stuff you need to know—and a lot of them are here to help you hook up to an attitude that ROCKS. An attitude that keeps you true to you! One that brings your deep-down ultracool self out from hiding for the world to see. An attitude that will let you SHINE!

1 What do you love about your life? **Write out a list of all the things you're thankful for!** It'll make you feel majorly blessed every time you look at it. Hang it up in your room as a constant reminder of the good stuff, or keep it folded in your drawer or purse and take it out whenever you need a lift. It sounds simple, but it's a nearly magical mood-booster!

2 BO got you bumming? When your body starts doing something new, it can feel like you're a freak of nature. Relax! You're not alone in this sweatfest. Puberty has some cool advantages, but with it comes some way-embarrassing stuff like excessive sweating from your armpits, hands, and even the soles of your feet. And since hormones are responsible for this sweat, it's likely to be the PU kind. To **keep your bod smelling as sweet as possible,** take a bath or shower every day. Use a strong deodorant, and carry it with you during the day for touch-up applications if neces-sary. If you sweat through your shirts a lot, consider bringing an extra one to school to change into after gym or dur-ing your lunch period. Avoid silk and light-colored fabrics that show sweat rings. If your sweating is really out of hand, go see your doc to make sure you don't have an infection.

TRY THIS! Shave your pits! Armpit hair traps the moisture from your sweat and makes a cozy spot for smelly bacteria to grow. You'll stay dry and smell sweeter longer if you're bare under there!

3 When you open your jewelry box, do you see a tangled web of silver, beading, gold, and string that only a surgeon could begin to unravel? Never fear! Your new organized self is here! Lots of crafts stores, tool stores, and even drugstores carry inexpensive sectioned boxes for things like buttons and screws. They work great to organize your jewelry! You can stack these plastic boxes in a drawer or even on your dresser. If you want to pretty them up, you can add contact paper to the outside edges, or glue fabric on them. You could also hang necklaces and bracelets from a man's tie rack, or from pushpins you push into the back of your closet door. And ice-cube trays make great ring and earring sorters!

TRY THIS!

If you're a jewelry hound and you're looking for cool ways to decorate your room, pin all your pins onto a white T-shirt you've outgrown and hang the tee right on your wall with a hook and a hanger! Hang a big, framed corkboard on your wall, too, and artfully arrange all your necklaces, bracelets, and rings so they dangle from pushpins. Your entire jewelry collection will be superaccessible, plus it'll be on display for you to enjoy every day!

Is there a celeb you can't stop thinking about? The dreamy guy in the last great flick you caught, or a diva whose heart-felt lyrics seem to speak to your very soul? Maybe it's an athlete or an author who inspires you to strive toward your personal best. Wouldn't it just blow your mind to be able to make a personal connection with your way-out-of-reach fave star? It's possible! Put your admiration into words and write a fan letter! Keep it short and simple and try to say something more original than "I just love you!" Most celebs have people who read their mail for them, but if your letter says something that makes it stand out from the rest, there's a chance the object of your affection will see it. Here are some ideas:

 Tell the songstress you love how she's made a diff in your life—maybe listening to her latest CD gave you the courage to patch things up with your dad, whom you hadn't spoken to in weeks. Stars love to hear about how they've had a positive influence on others.

 Ask a question in your letter. It will increase your odds of getting a response.

 Say how much you would treasure a signed photograph, and enclose an 8" x 10" envelope with your address and correct postage on it.

Type your letter and check and double-check it for spelling and grammar errors. Then see if you can find an address for your idol by searching the Internet or checking for a fan club in the association directories at your public library. Or, if your idol is a screen star, TV star, or recording artist, send your letter in care of the studio that made the star's most recent movie, show, or CD. For an author, send it to the publishing company that published the book you love. For a sports star, send it to the athlete's home stadium or wherever he or she plays. Then wait! Don't expect an answer right away, since celebs get a LOT of mail. And don't be heartbroken if you don't get a response at all—your lovin' words still may have met the eyes of your hero. Keep in mind that the very biggest stars—the ones on the cover of every current mag—are going to be the hardest to reach. If you can be a little original about who floats your boat— like if you notice a supercool pseudoceleb who's not in the spotlight big time right now—you'll stand a much better chance of getting a prompt, personal response.

5 **Make a commitment today to appreciate the here and now.** When you spend your time wishing, it's easy to focus all of your energies on the future. But once you get used to living that way, it will become a habit and you'll be eternally placing your happiness just out of your reach. Whatever is going on for you, NOW is the time to enjoy it, to celebrate it, to live it! If you keep thinking you'll be happy when a certain guy notices you, or when you make the swim team, or when your best friend gets back from her vacation, you're missing all the cool stuff in between. So look forward to those things happening, but DON'T WAIT for them to make you happy, or you'll rob yourself of the potentially mega-fun moment that you're living in! You will never be this exact age on this particular afternoon in this particular week of this month again in your whole life. How can you make the most of it?

6 **Make a scrapbook of your life.** Putting together a scrapbook is a fun present-moment activity that stretches your emotions into the past and will bring you lots of mushy moments in the future. Clean out your junk drawer, and fill a box with all the pictures, invitations, meaningful quotes and cards, clippings, etc., that spell out what your life is right now or has been for the past few months or years. Then pick out a sturdy album or scrapbook and arrange everything in chronological order. Paste it all in and write little notes about what you were thinking or feeling during each event. Make sure it's expandable so you can keep adding stuff as you become involved in more and more activities. Your scrapbook could soon become your most precious possession—a living, growing record of your fab life!

7 **Think for a minute about your current batch of buds.** Do you really, truly like them? It's pretty common for girls to try out several friendships or groups of friends before they find the best match for themselves. Sometimes a girl will fall into a group because she thinks they're popular and she feels lucky to be included. Maybe they don't make her feel that super about herself, but being part of their clique makes her feel more visible at school. If you enjoy *being seen* with your gal pals more than you actually enjoy *being with* them, they're probably not worth your time. If you were on a deserted island with these girls, there would be no one to see how cool you are. Would you enjoy their company, or are there some nicer girls you know that you'd rather be marooned with? If so, think about hooking up with the sweeter crowd.

TRY THIS!

If you notice a girl you'd like to get to know better, don't be afraid to make the first move. Ask her to study with you, or invite her over for some popcorn and a movie. She'll probably be flattered!

8 Do you have a personal style all your own? The more you make a point of knowing yourself, the more easily you'll **figure out the personal sense of style that works best for you.** Girls with real style don't just wear what the latest issue of their fave mag says is "in" or "hot" for that season—they choose clothes or accessories that express who they are and make them unique. Maybe you express your sunny disposition by carrying a bright yellow purse when everyone else's is brown or black. Maybe you always wear the beaded necklace that you strung yourself while on a special vacation you never want to forget. Maybe freedom of movement is especially important to you and you express it by wearing only comfortable pants and shoes when other girls are wearing confining skirts and clunky heels. The poet Emily Dickinson expressed her romantic nature by dressing entirely in white no matter the season. (This was during a time when it was fashionable to wear dark colors.) Style is more than just finding clothes that are flattering—it's finding a look that tells the world something about the person inside.

Been haunting the mall but having a hard time finding the look that expresses the true you? Or, when you find it, is your budget a total style-buster? Try junkin' it! You can find way-cool accessories and even clothes at garage sales, flea markets, and thrift shops. Maybe you think wearing preworn clothes is *grrrosss,* but hey!—a sudsy swirl in your washing machine is a fool-proof cootie-killer, and did you ever think about how many girls had tried on that dress you just paid megabucks for at the department store? You could even cop a save-the-world 'tude and congratulate yourself on your recycling habits. The trick to successful junkin' is to be extra-choosy even though the stuff is so cheap. Think mix 'n' match. That simple black scoop-neck tee for 10¢ doesn't look like much on its own, but paired with those purple checkered overalls for a quarter and that retro-cute hat for a buck, you've got a stylin' look for just $1.35. If you love something, but it's still a little pricier than you'd like, make an offer. Find out about weekend garage sales in Friday's newspaper and try to go early for the best selection (flea markets may be listed in the paper, too). Look in the yellow pages of the phone book for thrift and consignment shops. Plan to go with a bunch of pals—chances are, if you ask all the moms, at least one of them will think it's a cool idea and want to take you.

10 **Mix 'n' match your old stuff to give it new life!** Are you handy with a needle and thread? That stained blouse you're about to toss is sporting some fantastic buttons. See if those buttons fit through the buttonholes on the superplain, *so-last-year* sweater you're sick of. If they do, stitch up your own button transfer. You'll have a to-die-for sweater that your buds will be begging to borrow. Do this with your own old stuff, or be on the lookout for mix-'n'-match possibilities at garage sales and flea markets. You might even want to organize a swap with all your amigas. Be an artist and let the junk be your canvas!

11 Do you wish you were better at keeping in touch with far-away friends and family? **Take the plunge into cyberspace and find out who's got E-mail!** You could write a quick little paragraph each month describing what's going on in your life and E-mail it in a jiff to everyone on your need-to-catch-up-with list.

12 Don't you just love getting a real letter from someone? If E-mail isn't your thing, **be a holdout and join the preservation society for the nearly extinct art of letter-writing.** When you put your thoughts on paper and share them with someone you care about, you're giving that person a permanent keepsake of your unique relationship.

13 **If writing a letter seems like too much work, write notes!** Here's a supersimple way to keep a correspondence going: Address an envelope to your once-best gal pal who moved out of state and keep it in a handy spot on your dresser for a few weeks. Whenever you think of something you wish you could share with her, write her a note, like you used to do in school. Date it and drop it in the envelope. If you see a cartoon or quote she'd love, cut it out and add it to the notes. When the envelope is full, seal it, stamp it, and send it off! You could keep open envelopes for your favorite cousin, your sister in Maine, your pen pal . . . whoever.

Q & A Quickie

Question! Do I really have to write a thank-you note every time someone gives me a present? I never know what to say.

Answer! It's true that thank-you notes are becoming less commonplace, but they're still appreciated! Don't sweat the task, though—just a few nice words on a pretty piece of paper will get you off the hook. When you receive a cool thank-you note, save it so you can use it for inspiration when it's your turn. Or come up with one heartfelt phrase that expresses gratitude in your own personal way.

14 **Make the most of your energy curves!** Are you a morning girl or a night owl? It's a known fact that we all have times during the day when we're typically at our perkiest, and times when we're dragging our heels. These energy curves are called biological rhythms, and once you figure out what yours are, they can help you organize your day. Start paying attention to how you feel during those after-school hours. When you first get home, do you feel like crashing on the sofa, or do you have energy to spare? What about after dinner? Do you start to come alive then, or start to zone out? Make a commitment to tackle the stuff that requires the most concentration during those hours when you are most alert. Homework will be a lot easier and you'll get through it a lot faster if you do it when you're at the top of your curve. When you're at the low end of your curve, schedule activities that don't require as much concentration, like phone chats or cleaning your room. If you're planning an important conversation with a parent or pal, do it during one of your peak times! You can't do much to rearrange your school schedule, but becoming aware of your biological rhythms during your school day can help you combat those sluggish lulls. Try eating a small, high-energy snack like some nuts and have a few swigs of OJ as soon as you feel yourself starting to droop.

15 Do you put big school projects off until the last minute? Do you avoid cleaning your room until it's so messy it takes an entire weekend and four wheelbarrows to find your floor again? Can you say PROCRASTINATE? If you have a bunch of unfinished projects lying around and a to-do list longer than Santa's, you may be a procrastinator. Most people who procrastinate are just overwhelmed by the way they perceive a task. The job seems too big for them. They don't know where to start, so they just keep putting things off. If you can change the way you look at a project, you can end pro-crastination for good! Instead of seeing that school report as one big job, look at it as a bunch of little jobs. Instead of thinking, *Yikes! I have to write a report!* think, *I have to go to the library this afternoon and look for ideas for my report.* Then think, *I have to decide what my report will be about.* Then think, *I have to write an outline for my report.* Get it? Any job can be broken down into manageable components that make it seem a lot easier. If there's a task you especially hate, like cleaning your room, tell yourself that you're only going to do one part of it—whatever is easiest for you. Decide that this afternoon you will simply put away all of your clothes— that's all. Chances are, once you've breezed through that, you'll be on a roll and you'll want to go ahead and zip through the rest of it.

CAUTION CAUTION CAUTION CAUTION

TRY THIS!

Buddy up! Everything is more fun when you share it with a friend, so strik[e] a deal with your best am[igo] to share chores whenever possible. Maybe it's your job to rake the leaves in your yard, and your pal i[s] responsible for bathing h[is] family's enormous dog. Le[t] her rake with you for a f[ew] hours, then go hold her pooch in place while she lathers him up!

16 Don't confine yourself to always doing the same old thing.

Some of the most creative ideas come from "thinking outside the box," or looking at the regular stuff in our lives and trying to see it in different, more interesting ways. If your teachers are flexible, this kind of thinking can make your schoolwork a lot more fun. Let's say your class is assigned an oral report. Day after day, kids read

their *borrrring* book summaries to the half-snoozing class. But you thought outside the box when planning yours! You come to class dressed as Cleopatra, Queen of the Nile—the historic chick your report is about. You don't just drone off a few lame pages about the book you read. You recite a juicy love poem you wrote for your dreamboat, Marc Antony. You hang up a map of the domain you rule. You give your class a show to remember, and you naturally ace the assignment. Thinking outside the box can help you have fun with otherwise unfun stuff. Just make sure you follow your interests and throw yourself into it!

17 Will you be starting at a new school soon?

The first day can be freaky! Remember that everyone else in your grade will feel as lost as you do (unless you're new because of a move). Ask a lot of questions during orientation and read the student handbook so you'll know what to expect. Some schools allow visitors during the few days before classes start. If yours does, grab a buddy and go visit the maze in advance. Track down your locker and any classrooms you know you'll be in. You'll feel a lot more confident if you already have a clue where you're going on that first day. (If you can't get into your school until the day it starts, go super-early and do your detective work then!)

18 Can't keep your eyes open in history? Barely dragging your self from class to class? You're in an energy crisis! Here are some ways to **pump UP your energy level:**

 Make sure you get at least eight hours of Zs every night—more if you still have a hard time waking up in the morning.

 Drink plenty of water—dehydration can be an energy-zapper, so down those eight 8-ounce glasses every day (a stylish water bottle in your fave colors helps you commit to it).

★ Eat some protein at every meal, and try to cut back on sweets and white breads, which can lead to carbo-crashes that make you feel pooped.

★ Banish caffeine! It may pep you up for a moment, but it will ultimately drag you down, making you more sluggish than you were before you chugged it!

TRY THIS!

Protein-packed foods aren't the most convenient to grab in a jiffy. That's one reason so many of us carbo-load. Try individually wrapped string cheese for an easy protein and calcium boost! Or ask your mom to get you one of those fully cooked chickens that most grocery stores now carry in their deli sections. Pull all the meat off the bones and store the chunks of meat in an airtight container in the fridge. It's a gross job and your hands will get all slimy while you're at it, but then you'll have a few days' worth of delish little chicken pieces to snack on that are just as easy to snag as a handful of chips!

19 Exercise is great, but some girls make the mistake of doing too little or trying to do too much. **Pick an activity that you enjoy, and then set an exercise schedule that's easy for you to keep.** Try power-walking, blading, biking, swimming, or even dancing wildly in your room to your fave fast tunes! Are you shooting for every day, but feeling guilty when you skip now and then? Rather than beat yourself up, why not set your goal at four exercise sessions (a minimum of 20 minutes each) per week? You can always add in extra romps when you feel like it.

Q & A Quickie

Question! I'm very disciplined about exercise, but sometimes I can't last as long as I want to. No matter how hard I try, my body just gives out. How can I increase my stamina?

Answer! It sounds like your workout is too strenuous for you! If you're having trouble breathing, slow down, girlfriend! You should be breathing harder than normal but still be able to carry on a conversation. To increase stamina, go slowly. For now, stop working out when your body tells you to, but keep an eye on the clock and see if you can add a few more minutes each week. Also, be sure to warm up for five to ten minutes before you start exercising. The warm-up will increase your blood flow and heart rate, which will actually help you keep at it longer!

20 **When anyone pressures you to do anything that feels wrong to you, think about what's really going on.** Does he or she have your best interests at heart? NOT! Let's say a friend wants you to cut a class with her. Is it really your company she's after, or does she want someone to share the blame and punishment if she gets caught? What if your study-buddy convinces you to play video games when you had agreed to quiz one another for a test? Is he the least bit concerned about YOUR bad grade? Nope. And what about that jerk in the girls' room who keeps offering you a smoke? Is she being generous? NO WAY. She already knows she's made a big mistake, and she's trying to drag someone down with her. You don't need "friends" like this in your life. Ship 'em out!

21 Have you finally convinced Mom that you need some new duds to get you through the school year? Have the two of you set a date to shop, but the prospect of haggling with her over every purchase makes you only semipsyched about the outing? Do some advance planning to make sure your shopping day goes smoothly.

TRY THIS!
If you need to find pants to match that multicolored plaid shirt you love, snip a tiny piece of the shirt's fabric from an inside seam. (Don't get too close to the stitching, or you'll soon have a hole!) Tape the little piece of fabric to a white index card and bring it with you so you can find just the right color to go with your shirt.

First, narrow down what you really, really want to a few items. Let Mom know before the shopping day that there are a couple of things you totally have your heart set on, and you're counting on her help and advice for the other purchases. Then blow her away with your so-responsible shopping smarts by making a list of what you already have. Make a second list of things you could add to make the most of your existing wardrobe. Maybe you're sick of the embroidered butterflies on the shirt that's part of your navy skirt set, but the navy skirt is still way-flattering. A too-cute white top could give it a whole new life!

22 Is your bod growing faster than the weeds in your yard? Puberty can come on slowly, or it can hit you like an asteroid! Sometimes the rapid growth of your body can make you temporarily a little klutzy, so if you find yourself knocking stuff over and bumping into things, don't panic. It's just a little temporary uncoordination between your eyes and limbs. When a girl grows (especially a tall girl), her familiarity with her body sometimes has trouble keeping up with its growing size. So when she reaches for a glass of OJ, her brain might tell her it's farther away than it actually is. This is because her brain is used to her arm being 20 inches long, and suddenly her arm is 25 inches long. Oops! Spillage! It doesn't happen to everyone, but if it's happening to you, it can make you feel majorly awkward! Now that you know it's just another normal-yet-bizarre part of becoming a teen, you can beat it! It sounds crazy to have to practice reaching for stuff, but that's the best way to get graceful again. Just keep your little dilemma in mind and make your moves slowly. If you can slow down and concentrate a little more on all those movements you've been taking for granted, you'll be poised and confident again in no time.

23 Meditation is a supercool way to keep a healthy head. See if you can block off 10 minutes of each day for meditation practice. Sit or lie down, or get into any position that's comfortable for you. Concentrate on your breathing and try to keep your mind as empty as you can. Stay focused in the present moment, where your worries about tomorrow and regrets about yesterday can't touch you! You'll feel your body relaxing and a sense of peacefulness engulfing you. After about 10 minutes of focusing on nothing but your breathing, allow your mind to drift to whatever is happening with you. You may find you're able to get a better, wiser grasp on your probs when you're in this state of mind.

24 Learn to play an instrument! It's fun, it can lead you to new friends, and it can even make you smarter. Did you know that students who sing or play an instrument score 51 points higher on SATs than the national average? To be good at anything requires discipline, but once you get hooked on the feeling of creating music, you'll look forward to each practice session. Playing an instrument is a great activity that lets you forget about everything else for a while. It can be a totally cool mood-booster!

2.5 Are you a tin-grin, metal-mouth, brace-face—you know…do you wear braces? If you do, you've probably heard all of the above nicknames. Aren't they cute? And it's oh-so-clever of those dearies who dream them up for you, isn't it? As if the aggravation of wearing the bleepin' things wasn't bad enough! We're not going to kid you—there's no fun side to braces—at least not while you've got them on. And it's hard to take comfort in knowing that you REALLY will be glad you had them when they come off. (But you will!) To make the most of your temporarily "decorated" grin, concentrate your efforts on the rest of your face and bod. Use pretty clips in your hair and wear a cool necklace. Whatever YOU give your attention to is what others will notice about you. So if you're always thinking about your braces, they'll stick out a lot more than they will if you can just forget about them. Look around—tons of kids your age are sporting them. Maybe even some supercute guy you'll sit next to in the waiting room when you go for your next ortho appointment!

2.6 Do you think you're too fat? Surveys have shown that most teenage and preteen girls answer yes to that question when they are actually the perfect weight for their body type! If you compare yourself to actresses and models, you're setting yourself up to be mega-disappointed with your bod. A more realistic approach to judging your weight is to compare yourself to the REAL girls you see in school. (Yes, all of them—not just the skinniest ones!) If you're heavier than most of them, and you find yourself out of breath after physical activity like walking up stairs briskly, you might want to think about setting some healthy weight-loss goals for yourself. But if you feel energetic and healthy, chances are, you're just being too critical of your body. Try different clothing styles to find your most flattering look, then commit to loving yourself just as you are!

27 **If you determine that you really do need to lose some weight, stop complaining about it and DO IT!** You have the power to be anything you want to be, and YOU control the size of your body. You'll have the best success if you ask an experienced adult to help you set a realistic goal for your-self and plan a sensible weight-loss program. If you don't want to ask your mom or another family member, try the school nurse. Remember these three mega-crucial rules: 1. How much you put into your mouth is not nearly as important as WHAT you put into it. 2. Exercise! 3. Go s-l-o-w-l-y. (The faster you lose weight, the more likely you'll be to put it right back on.) Learn how many calories are in your favorite foods, and replace them with low-cal options. If you stick to fresh, healthy foods, you can shed pounds without ever feeling hungry. Find an exercise that you really enjoy and get on a regular program. Losing extra weight can make you feel great, but be sure to stop when you hit your goal. Then figure out what you need to eat and do in order to keep your weight right where it is.

TRY THIS!

Remember how much you loved being active before you started calling it "exercise"? Staying fit doesn't have to be drudgery. Skip rope, hop on a trampoline, or play "hot potato" while you jump around with your friends. Let loose and be a kid again!

28 **Teen mags can be fun, but don't believe those bogus ads!** It's bad enough when ads push you to buy products you don't need, but it's mega-gnarly when the whole ad is a big fat lie. If you come across an ad for any of those products that promise to melt pounds off you and quickly and easily reshape your entire body, rip out the page and make a paper air-plane out of it. These ads typically feature a skinny, beaming girl in a tiny bikini with lots of quotes about how fantastic her life is now that she's thin, thanks to this amazing product. IT IS FICTION. If such a product truly existed, it would be on the evening news, not in the back of a teen magazine. The ad is written so that you can't tell what the mysterious product actually is. (In most cases, the "product" is just printed instructions on how to diet and exercise.) They tell you to send money (not a check) and assure you that the package that comes to you will not offer any clue as to what's inside. They claim this is for your privacy, but it is really because they know that if your parents found out you were wasting money on their garbage, they could get into big trouble. These companies are targeting you because they think teen girls are insecure about their weight and stupid enough to fall for their gimmick. SHOW THEM THAT THEY'RE WRONG!

29 We know you've heard all about eating disorders and that you think nothing like that could ever happen to you. But every girl who's now suffering from anorexia nervosa or bulimia once had that same belief. Sadly, we live in a time and place that glorifies unnatural thinness in women. It hasn't always been that way and it won't always be that way, but for right now, we're stuck with it. YOU can make a choice to not be a victim. Be proud to have a REAL girl's bod. Make a promise to yourself, right now, that you will never endanger your health in order to lose weight. Girls who become obsessed with diet and exercise are no fun to be around, and they have no fun themselves. A lot of them become very, very sick and many die. If you're afraid it may be happening to you or someone you know, call the Eating Disorder Hotline for help (1-800-248-3285).

30 Get back at those advertisers! If you're peeved at the way women are portrayed in ads, don't just gripe to your gal-pals about it. Make your voice heard! Next time you're cruisin' the net, log on to http://www.edap.org (Eating Disorders Awareness & Prevention). This cool site has a Watchdog program that lets you sign your name to monthly cyberletters that are sent to advertisers who contribute to negative images of women. Yeah!

31 Tune in to your inner power! Some girls think *power* is a negative word. They don't want to get wrapped up in "power struggles," and they feel it is unfeminine to want to have power. But power doesn't have to mean power over other people. In fact, when you feel truly powerful within yourself, you have no need or desire to try to change or control anyone else. Inner power is knowing that YOU control your reactions to whatever life hands you; you have the power to be and do whatever you want; you have the power to love others completely, without looking for anything in return. People who don't feel powerful within themselves are the ones who try to control others.

32 Get your duds in a row. Ever spend 20 minutes searching for your cutest tee, only to find it hopelessly wrinkled from sharing tight quarters with 35 of your less-fave articles of clothing? Wish your clothes were more organized? All it takes is a little planning! Set your closet up according to four simple categories. First, group everything you wear on the top half of your body—shirts, sweaters, jackets, T-shirts, tanks—and hang them together in one section of your closet. Next, group together everything you wear on the bottom half, like jeans, pants, and skirts. After that, make a smaller section for whole-body clothes like dresses and overalls, and finally, leave the toughest-to-reach corner for your dressiest duds that don't see too much action. If your clothes are crammed in so tight you need a crowbar to remove a hanger, pare down! Pass everything that no longer fits (plus all that stuff that you just never wear) to a younger sis or cousin, or give it to a charity. Ask your mom to designate a place in the house for your out-of-season clothes so they don't clutter up your closet. Those big plastic trash cans with lids work great if the only extra storage space you've got is in a musty basement or garage. Make sure the lid is snapped all the way on for an airtight fit. Even if they don't require hanging, keep as many of your favorite things as you can in your closet. Clothes in drawers tend to get forgotten about or wrinkled.

33 Girls go through a lot of weird crud as they mature. But ya know what? So do boys. At least you can count on your voice being loyal to you. A guy can go to bed sounding pretty much like he always did and wake up sounding like a cross between Mickey Mouse and some way-bad Elvis impersonator. We only mention this in a book for girls because we want you to be kind to the poor guys. Boys get a lot of unwanted attention for their voice changes. A guy will mega-appreciate a girl who ignores certain cracks and earsplitting squeaks while he's trying to converse with her. In other words, DO NOT dissolve into giggles and run and tell all your friends when he seems to morph into Kermit the Frog. Show him the same kindness that you'd want him to show you if your emergency maxi-pad fell out of your purse onto his feet. Puberty isn't easy on anyone!

34 Do you have a superstar sib? Are you afraid you'll never live up? It's hard not to compare yourself to your brothers and sisters, especially when one of them does something that makes your parents really proud. Maybe your older brother is a megahero on the tennis team, and you see how much attention and praise that gets him. That could easily make you want to perfect your backhand and try out for the team, too, but put the brakes on those tennis shoes for a minute! Is swinging a racket really your passion? If you follow exactly in his footsteps, the comparisons will never end! Become a star in YOUR OWN show. There are scads of sports, hobbies, and achievements that your folks will applaud just as much as tennis. Search out the one that lets YOU shine!

35 Be happy with who you are and live your life with integrity. Girls with integrity have figured out what their personal code of conduct is, and they stick to it, no matter what! They aren't swayed by the crowd, and they don't get "carried away by the moment" to do things they'll later regret. Having integrity means knowing and respecting yourself—and nothing could make you more attractive!

CATCH THE BUZZ!

Actor Kirk Cameron says, "Personally, I never set out to be the best actor in the world, nor did I set out to be rich or famous. For me, I am setting out to have integrity."

36 If you want to get more shine out of your strands, leave 'em alone!

Hair that gets too much attention—from perms, colors, curling tools, or too many hair products like gels and sprays—will break and get dull a lot faster than hair that gets simple TLC. Wash with a gentle everyday shampoo and use a conditioner only if your hair is dry. (If it's oily at the roots but dry at the ends, just use conditioner on the ends.) Then gently towel-dry your hair and let it dry on its own, or use a blow-dryer on the coolest setting to dry it just halfway.

Quick Q & A

Question! I can't wait to experiment with different do-it-yourself hair dyes, but my mom is totally NO WAY about it. What should I do?

Answer! Go give her a big smooch and say thanks! Hair dyes you use at home are often complete disasters. The color may not look anything like the picture on the box, your hair could get damaged, and you'd become a slave to root touch-ups! Even professional dye jobs you get in salons can be unpredictable.

37 You don't have to turn into a chem head to have fun with hair color. Try a natural beautifier.

Even the strictest moms are usually cool with a little food play. Try squeezing the juice of a whole lemon onto your wet head and combing it through your locks. Slather sunscreen on your body and relax in the sunshine for about half an hour. When you wash the lemon out, you may notice shimmery golden highlights that look a lot more natural than the painted-on kind! If your hair is dark, you can get the same effect with chamomile tea. Dunk two bags into a cup of boiling water and let the stuff cool off. Then soak your strands in the tea and cover them up in a shower cap for about half an hour. Wash the tea out and admire the gleam! (Some girls will have to repeat the steps a few times to get noticeable results.)

38 Pick flowers! Don't nab your elderly neighbor's prizewinning tulips, but any old wildflowers you see in a field or your own yard are fine. Pick them for a pal who's feeling down; for your mom, to say sorry for being such a typical teenage daughter sometimes; or—if you're feeling confident and crazy enough—for a guy you like!

39 Have you been itching to redecorate your room? Your personal space says a lot about you, and as fast as you're changing, your room may be lagging behind! Instead of going out and buying a batch of new-digs-gear that you may later regret, **try this decorating trick**: Take EVERYTHING down—even the stuff you know you'll want to keep. Make your walls bare, make your dresser bare. Put every single ceramic poodle and stuffed crocodile into a big box in the basement for one week. Living with all that emptiness will open up your creative self to all kinds of new possibilities. You may find a welcome sense of peacefulness in a room devoid of clutter. If your parents are cool with it, slap a fresh coat of color on your walls. After one week, unpack the boxes and see what you love in them. Find the just-right spot for each of your fave things. Chances are good that there will be plenty left in the boxes to pack up or get rid of. Once you have your most cherished art and objects in their new and perfect places, you may decide your redecorating is finished. If not, buy new stuff slowly, one thing at a time. If you rush and fill up all the empty spots, there won't be any wall space left for that fab poster you'll see three months from now. If you take your time decorating it, your room will have a chance to grow and evolve *with you*.

40 If you wear prescription glasses, do you love 'em or hate 'em? **If you don't love your specs, wake up, girl!** Glasses are so cool that lots of people who don't even need them wear them for the fashion fun of it. And there are so many cute and flattering frames to choose from! If you stop treating your glasses as a necessary evil, they could become

your favorite accessory—a major part of your individual style. If the glasses you have now don't float your boat, let your parents know you'd like to select new ones. You may have to put them on a wish list for a holiday or your birthday, since cool specs don't come cheap. But don't you think it's worth forfeiting whatever other gifts you might have gotten, since you put the things on your face every day? If you're a real fashion freak, maybe you could even snag two pairs to reflect your different moods on different days.

41 Every time you claim something is not your fault, you lose personal power, so **take responsibility!** If you don't like something, you can change it, but only if you first own up to it. Say you fail your science test and your mom is giving you a hard time about it. "It's not my fault!" you wail. "The teacher didn't explain the stuff well enough, and then she made the test too hard!" Chances are good you're not too happy with yourself for having failed the test. And if the grade was truly "not your fault," then you would be completely powerless to prevent it from happening again. But when you take responsibility, you gain POWER over the situation. You can put it behind you and plan strategies for preventing it the next time around. For example, you could go to the teacher for extra help if you don't understand what's being taught.

42 Isn't it fun when you spot a brand-new boy-babe who makes your heart go flippity-flop? You get all excited every time you see him in the hall, in class, or even when he's just a tiny speck on the opposite end of the bleachers at the assembly! Face it—having a crush on a guy you've never said boo to can be a super mood-booster! In your mind, you can make him be whatever kind of person you want him to be. Go ahead and do this kind of crush as often as you'd like. There's just one important REALITY CHECK to remember: Attempting to make this stranger an actual boyfriend would be a major magic-zapper. There is no way this real-life guy could ever be a fraction as primo as the pretend guy you've imagined him to be. Enjoy looking at the flesh-and-bones version, but let the relationship live in the place it was born—your head!

13 Are you tired of crushing from afar? Are you looking to claim someone as your actual, very own boyfriend? Be CHOOSY. You can enjoy a just-for-kicks crush on anyone, but you can't let just any boy into your heart! There are guys your age who would make supercool boyfriends, but not all of them are up to the task. It takes practice to spot a guy who's special enough to wear the label of your BF.

14 Does the boy you're crushing on like you back? For some weird reason, lots of girls waste tons of effort and tears on guys who just don't return their lovin' feelings. Dumb! Here's how to tell if the boy you like likes you: When you see him, smile. Does he ever smile back? If he does, then start a conversation with him. Ask him what the math homework was or if he's going to the football game. After you've started the first conversa-tion, wait. If he likes you, he'll start the next one (unless he's particularly shy—in which case you might want to start a few more conversations to make sure he knows you're interested). It's that simple!

TRY THIS!

When you're confused about whether or not a boy likes you, think about that rule from science class: For every action, there's an equal reaction (or something like that). If you're doing all the actions and you're not getting an equal reaction, MOVE ON! Don't waste time pining away for a boy who is obviously wrong for you

45 OK, so let's say you know for certain that he's interested in you. Don't start celebrating yet! Instead, begin your investigation. You still need to find out how dating-worthy he is. Most girls don't realize this, but JUST BECAUSE YOU CHOOSE TO GET TO KNOW HIM BETTER, IT DOESN'T MEAN YOU HAVE TO GO OUT WITH HIM. It's OK to show interest in a guy and then change your mind about him if he turns out to be less fab than you expected.

46 Wondering how you can get to know a boy better? Ask him to hang with you and your friends for a casual event you'd be going to anyway, like a sports competition at your school. Or ask him to work on a class project with you, or study together for a test. If he likes you, he'll probably agree to almost anything you suggest, or maybe he'll have his own suggestions. When you're together, ask him lots of questions about himself. Most boys love that, and it's the best way for you to find out if the two of you are compatible. Does he like doing the same things you like to do? Does he seem to share your values? Does he make you laugh? Is he interested in what you have to say? Does he make you feel good about yourself? If you answered yes to these questions, he's passed the BF test.

Question! I like a boy and I'm pretty sure he likes me, too, but we haven't really hung out together yet. Is it OK for me to ask him out, and if it is, what should I ask him to do?

Answer! Of course you can ask him out! No relationship is any good without honesty. Ask him to join you and your buds in doing anything you would normally do. If he truly is cool, he'll be happy to do lots of things, in groups or alone with you, such as play board games, exercise, go to museums, do homework, go out for ice cream, hang out at the library, go bowling or skating, walk through the mall, bake cookies, play tennis, or just sit on a park bench, talking. All of that stuff can be awesome when you do it with a really special guy!

Q u i c k i e
& A

47 A guy is definitely NOT cool enough to be your boyfriend if he doesn't want anyone to know the two of you are an item. He is NOT cool enough if he only wants to be with you in places where he might get you to make out with him. He's NOT cool enough if he ever makes you feel bad about yourself in any way. He's NOT cool enough if he pressures you to do ANYTHING AT ALL that you don't want to do. If the guy you're with starts fitting that description, do not wait another second before you dump him. No matter how great he once seemed, he's no longer worthy of the role of your BF.

48 So you have this great boyfriend and everything is just peachy. Realize that you will break up. "What?!" you scream. Well, sorry to have to tell you, but it's a fact of life. That wonderful BF you dig so much right now will probably at some point be nothing more to you than a (hopefully sweet) memory. People break up. Young people who are just starting to date break up even more. Maybe you'll break up with him and maybe he'll break up with you, but either way, it's nothing to rip through a box of tissues over. You may be sad, mad, or glad, but whatever you feel, it will pass. There are lots of cutie-pies out there, and as long as you make sure each one of them passes the date-worthiness test, you will have buckets of exciting dating experiences ahead of you. Try to get through breakups without making enemies—boys are people, too, and chances are, you'll run into each ex-boyfriend many times before you finish school. Wouldn't it be cooler to be able to smile and say hello than to be constantly ducking behind your best friend until he passes?

49 Maybe you want to have a bona fide, ultracool boyfriend, but you don't know how to get one. Stop looking for him! The weird truth is that the more you can forget about boys and be happy with all the stuff going on in your life that has nothing to do with them, the more attractive you become to them! A girl who's loving life and feeling proud of who she is will never fail to get noticed by the very coolest guys. It's an attitude that's irre-sistible. When a girl sees herself as totally fab, guys will see her that way, too. But you can't fake it. The girls who are faking it are the ones everyone calls conceited. When you truly like yourself, you don't have to put anyone else down. You're kind and friendly and you want to help others be as happy as you are. That's the kind of girl who shines. That's the kind of girl boys fall head over heels for.

50 As much as you love hanging with your buds, don't forget to set aside some time just for yourself. Alone-time is really important, and with all you've got going on, it can be hard to find a peaceful, quiet moment to just BE. When you're feeling a little overwhelmed by the world, tell the family to take your phone messages, put your DO NOT DISTURB sign on your door, and just chill. Doing nothing by yourself is one of the best ways to truly relax your mind, body, and soul.

51 If you're working hard toward a goal, don't forget to celebrate each small step that takes you closer to it. It's easy to be so focused on the finish line that we forget to enjoy the race! If you're training for a big gymnastics competition and your routine isn't perfect yet, get psyched about the fact that you get better every single time you practice. Even if all you're doing is trying to grow out your nails— every morning when you wake up, they're longer than they were the day before, so start the day smiling!

CATCH THE BUZZ!

Famous spiritual author Deepak Chopra says, "Success is . . . a journey and not a destination."

52 Do you have any idea how many TV commercials have wig-gled their way into your poor brain over the past decade or so? The main message behind a lot of them is always the same:

You're not good enough the way you are, but you'd be perfect if you'd only buy/use/do whatever it is they're selling. **Don't fall for advertisements!** The people in the commercials are actors who have probably never even used the products they're saying are so wonderful! Smart girls recognize most ads for what they are: FAKE!

53 Are you secretly dying to feel the thrill of performing onstage but too chicken to audition? **Get your feathered tail over there and try out for the school play!** And don't just read for the part of Woman on Corner, whose only line is, "He went that way, Officer!" Read for the lead! You may not get it, but your performance could still land you that Woman on Corner role, and who knows—maybe you'll get a kickin' part that's somewhere in between.

CATCH THE BUZZ!

Comedian David Brenner says, "When I was thirteen years old, I said to my mother, 'I'm shooting for the highest star up there, Mom, because if I miss, the worst that'll happen is I'll fall onto the moon, but if I aim for the moon and miss, I'm liable to land right back in the neighborhood.'"

54 Does your dad look at you like you're some bizarre stranger visiting the house these days? Dads can have a tough time when their little girls start morphing into actual women. Because he's secretly ga-ga for you (trust us on this one), Dad is apt to be a little protective during this time in your life. He may forget to remind you that the reason behind his rules, curfews, and nearly postal reactions to your wardrobe is that he cares about you (duh!). The more you rant, bolt, and slam doors, the more WORRIED and out of control he's gonna feel. So stay cool, girl! **Talk to Dad one-on-one** (unless Mom is your ally—then count her in) and explain that the changes that you are going through have been inevitable since the day you were born. He may be feeling sad inside about losing Daddy's little girl, so tell him that you love him as much as ever and you need his friendship and support now. Most of all, clue him in to what's up with you. If communication is open, he won't have as much to wonder about and freak over.

55 There are a few certain clothing brand names (you know what they are) that are humongously popular right now. But take a good look at the stuff itself. Would you ever pay attention to it if it didn't have that popular name on it? Don't get sucked into buying everything the advertisers tell you is completely necessary for your continued existence on this planet. It's all bogus! Smart girls figure out which styles and colors look best on them, and that's what they buy and wear, no matter what the labels say. Anyone can follow a trend—be someone who SETS them!

CATCH THE BUZZ!

American statesman Ben Franklin said, "Joy is not in things. It is in us."

56 Do you get the once-a-year, spring-time, bathing suit blues? No matter how much you accept and love yourself, those first few days of wearing next-to-nothing can melt your bod-confidence big time! When you're shopping for a bathing suit, be prepared to spend a lot of time trying on different styles (at least more time than you'd spend when you're shopping for a new sweater). And even if you figured out the perfect style for you last year, your curves may have undergone

some major changes over the winter, so keep an open mind! Once you find a suit you love, do a few of your wildest dance moves in the dressing room. You want to make sure that nothing's gonna play peekaboo in the middle of that beach volleyball game or during pool-play with that cute lifeguard. Most of all, be kind to yourself and remember that practically every girl you'll see at the pool or beach this year is going through the same pre-season agony!

TRY THIS!

If you're just yearning for bigger-looking yahoos, get a suit with underwire—some even have removable push-up pads! Or try pairing a horizontally striped, tank-style top with skimpier solid-colored bottoms. For the opposite problem (yahoos you'd rather tone down than play up), go for a sport top with plenty of coverage. If your figure is still more straight and boyish than you'd like, try a one-piece with cutouts along the sides of the waistline. Or go for a bikini in bright colors or a busy print. Emphasizing the places you'd like to be curvier will make you seem less straight (the more fabric the better!). If you're not wild about your thighs, try one of those adorable skirt-suits (or look for suits cut high along the legs to elongate and thin the appearance of your thighs). For a too-thick middle, try a one-piece with side stripes. And if your back is beauteous but your abs don't make the cut, focus attention where you want it by choosing a simple but totally back-baring one-piece.

57 Summer can be brutal on your hair. When those first few humid days surprise you with a wicked case of the frizzies, get into gear with some countermoves. That super-poufed-out look is from moisture that has gotten into your hair cuticle and made it swell. Spritz your locks with some water, rub a little gel in your hands, smooth it over your hair, and let it air dry. To prevent the frizz biz in the first place, try one of those antifrizz products that you use after washing your hair.

58 If you're blonde and you get that groovy green glow after swimming, try these tricks to **get golden again**: First, use a good clarifying shampoo to wash the chlorine out. Then start drenching your hair completely in fresh, clean water *before* you take a dip. The clean water will keep your hair from absorbing the stuff in pools that gets it green. For mega-protection of your strands, comb conditioner through your wet hair and leave it in during all your water-play.

59 When you're feeling like a crank . . . crank up the music! Not that weirdly pop-ular hate/anger/in-your-face music—what are you trying to do, leap headfirst into a cesspool of depression? We're talking about GOOD music that LIFTS your spirits instead of beating them  against a brick wall. Come on, you know you've got some . . . there's at least one CD in your collection that makes you smile every time you flip by it. Play your favorite track and belt out the words with all your might. Singing is a supercool and often-overlooked outlet for emotional release. In other words, it makes you feel good.

60 Are you itching for hairless gams? Think twice before you pick up that razor! It's true that most American females start shaving their legs at some point in their lives, but why is that exactly? For some ridiculous reason, someone way back when decided that we look better that way. But unless you enjoy being a slave girl to your beauty, put it off as long as you can. The hairs on your legs are probably really fine and nice-looking right now. Once you shave them JUST ONCE, they'll never be that way again. They'll come back stubby and thicker and kinda yuck, and then you'll have a *reason* to shave 'em. Do you really want to have to spend that extra five to ten minutes in the bathroom every time you wear a gam-baring out-fit? Isn't there something more fun you could do with your time? If you think hairless legs will make you more attractive to the guys, guess again. Guys are clueless about girly stuff like that. Being confident and loving your whole natural self is what makes guys notice you. And even though shaving's a pain, it's still a lot easier than any of the alternatives like waxing (can you say OUCH!!!?) or depilatories (supersmelly foams and creams that disintegrate your leg hairs, and then you have to wait a million years before you can do it again, during which time your legs look ugly).

61 You may be starting to wonder just how much maintenance your now-womanly crotch area is going to require. If you believe the ads, or if you're unfortunate enough to stumble across the feminine hygiene aisle in your drugstore, you could get the idea that it's a full-time job. Don't buy into it! Leave your privates alone. Companies will go to great lengths to convince you that you need special deodorants, douches, and powders to cover up the perfectly natural down-there scents that no one in the world will ever notice anyway. Some of this stuff is downright dangerous! Douching can lead to nasty infections by messing up your normal pH balance, and powders and sprays can cause rashes. Your daily soap-and-water routine is the ONLY attention your "snush" (that's what our mom called it) needs. If some pubic hairs are really sticking out of your swimsuit, go ahead and shave them (carefully!) with a good shaving gel or cream. It can be itchy when they grow back, so save those bikini-line shaves for times when you know you'll be suiting up.

62 Being nice to other people is totally together, but being nice to yourself is crucial! Listen to that little voice inside your head for a minute—is it a friendly voice or does it constantly tell you what an idiot you are? If it can't be polite, evict it! (No, we haven't gone coco-loco with this one—this is important stuff!) Every time you hear that little voice saying bad things about you, remember that YOU are in control of it. Reprogram the stubborn thing to treat you better, because whatever it says about you is likely to become the truth.

CATCH THE BUZZ!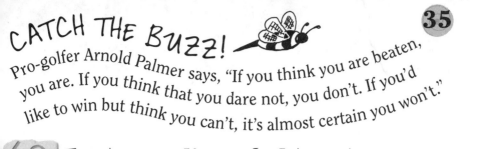

Pro-golfer Arnold Palmer says, "If you think you are beaten, you are. If you think that you dare not, you don't. If you'd like to win but think you can't, it's almost certain you won't."

63 Treat yourself or a bud to a stress-zappin' massage session.

Massage has been around practically forever as a pain-reliever, energy-booster, blues-buster, and all-around good thing. It enhances your awareness of your bod (in a good way!), banishes tension, and restores flexibility to tight, sore muscles. It can even improve your posture and help your system get rid of nasty toxins. Your library has a bunch of books that will clue you in to the best techniques.

TRY THIS!

Is Mom pooped from a tough day at work? Treat her to this little massage teaser: Take her hand and hold it gently for a few minutes. Then, supporting her palm with your fingers, make circular motions with your thumbs from the base of her fingers to her wrist. Still supporting her palm with your fingers, slide your thumbs and the heels of your hands from the center to the sides of her hand. Next, use your thumb and index finger to pull along the length of each finger, right to the tips. Give a little squeeze the tip of each finger. Take hold of her thumb between your thumb and forefinger. Massage the base with your heel and fingertips. Press into the web of flesh between her thumb and forefinger. Finally, turn her hand over and support it on your thigh or in your hand. Make sure her elbow is flexed. Make small, circular movements of your thumbs over her palm, moving gradually up to stroke her wrist. Instant feel-good...and that was just a hand!

64 Ever wake up from a too-weird dream and say "Huh?" If you know how to hash them out, dreams can offer major insights into the true you. According to Phyllis Koch-Sheras, Ph.D., and Amy Lemley, authors of *The Dream Sourcebook,* "Your dreaming mind has access to information about yourself that is not readily available to your waking mind." Even if you don't pay any attention to them, dreams help you cope with your everyday stuff. The best way to help your dreams help you is to keep a notebook by your bed and write everything down that you can remember about your dream. Focus on the way the different parts of your dream made you feel. Don't worry about sequence or whether or not anything makes sense. Just record the images and how you felt about them. Then think about what in your real life makes you feel the same way—that's how you decode your dream symbols. If you dreamt about a big scary dog that made your gut tense up, think, *What else makes my gut tense up like that?* Is there a growly brother or friend who's been "barking" at you? Maybe in the dream you yelled back at the dog and it slunk away, leaving you feeling proud and victorious. That could be your unconscious mind telling you you're ready to stand up to your real-life intimidator. Whenever you're stuck trying to figure out a dream, just take a guess. Even if you doubt you're right, relax and guess *something*. Your guesses will usually be more right than you think because guesses come from your unconscious—the same place your dreams come from. Most of all, don't overthink your dreams and don't worry about them. With or without your help, they really are hard at work, sorting out your stuff.

65 Longing for longer locks? When your aim is to go from long to short, you can get a great new do in a jiff. But when you're starting with short and you're dreaming of long, you've got to make the best of some less-than-fab in-between time! Don't stay away from your stylist when you're growing out your hair. Let her know your goal, but go in for your regular trims so your hair won't get too yuck while it's

growing out. She'll probably have suggestions—
like layering or cutting bangs—according to
your long-term plans. Experiment with cute
little clips, skinny headbands, chic low
ponytails, and cool hats.

66 Does it seem to you that no one knows the meaning
of MANNERS anymore? Kids cut in front of you in line,
practically knock you over in the hallways, and make obnoxious
comments over nothing! Before you get all freaked out over it,
take a deep breath. People are rude for a lot of reasons that have
nothing to do with you. Instead of taking it personally,
just return rudeness with perfect poise and
politeness. You'll be the better person and you'll walk away
liking yourself instead of wondering how they got YOU to be a
swine as well.

CATCH THE BUZZ!
Etiquette maven Emily Post says, "Manners are a sensitive
awareness of others. If you have the awareness, you have good
manners, no matter what fork you use."

67 Do you love the thought of the upcoming school dance
except for that little word it's all based on: *dance*? If the
mere idea of shakin' your groove thang in front of anyone besides
your dog makes you break out in a sweat, you're not alone. How
many chances do you think any of your classmates have had to pub-
licly bust a move? Take a deep breath, grab some buds
for safety in numbers, and bop your bootie off!
If you're laughing and enjoying yourself, everyone will think that
whatever steps you're swingin' in are the latest moves. (If you're
really freaking, just watch everyone else for a few minutes and do
what they're doing.)

68 Worried that no guy will ask you to dance at the big school shindig? Worried even more that one WILL? Either way, it's no biggie. Dancing with girlfriends is as grooving as anything, but if your night won't be complete without some boy-time, pick one and ask him yourself. If he says no, there's no need to crawl under the punch-bowl table. He has as much right to decline an offer as you do. Ask someone else! If you get asked by a boy you like, major boogie bonus! Don't be afraid he won't dig your dancing; he's probably worrying about the same thing. Just follow his motions, or gently lead him to follow yours. And even if the guy who's asked you isn't your dreamboat, go ahead anyway—it's only a dance. Pull a girlfriend onto the floor with you and make it a threesome if you're afraid he'll get the wrong idea. If you must turn him down, do it with kindness. It took guts for him to ask!

CATCH THE BUZZ!

Nobel Peace Prize–winner Mother Teresa said, "Kind words can be short and easy to speak, but their echoes are endless."

69 Want to tone up, flex your stuff, and feel fab? Learn yoga! It's like an exercise and a meditation all in one. Yoga uses stretching and breathing techniques to keep your body firm and lean, your mind clear and calm, and your spirit soaring.

Check out the yellow pages for classes in your area, or check out some books from the library to get you started.

70 When your parents just don't get you and you're feeling like you must have been switched at birth, think: grandparents. They're even older so they must be even more uncool, right? Wrong! Grandparents can be surprisingly sympathetic to the teen cause. For one thing, they can view you a little more objectively than your parents can because they didn't personally raise you and therefore aren't as inclined to think of you as an extension of themselves. For another, they've raised teenagers before and seen them go on to become adults. They probably know a few things that your parents don't about letting go and trusting that all will turn out well. Plus, all that experience that old people accumulate really is worth something. Your folks might be a little peeved that you can talk to *their* parents when you don't want to talk to *them,* but they'll also be relieved that there's someone in the family who's helping you. The most important thing is to make sure you have a reliable place to go to for adult guidance. If your grandparents don't make the cut, try out an aunt or uncle or friend's mom until you make a strong connection.

71 When homework gets really tough, or you're suddenly scratching your head and saying, "I just don't get it!" don't wait for things to improve on their own! Go see your teacher. Your teach will respect you for the effort, and you'll feel a

TRY THIS!
Organize a study group with people in your class that you respect. Working together can help yc stay on top of a subject, ar sometimes several heads are better than one. Just don' limit your study group to best buds—you don't want whole thing to turn into big gabfest!

lot better if you get a handle on the tough stuff before you get too far behind.

72. Parties are primo, but think twice before you accept an invitation from someone you don't know. Face it—if you don't know the person who's throwing the party, you have no idea what to expect when you get there. Play it safe and stay away. You'll have plenty of chances to get down and boogie in places where you feel happy and comfortable.

73. Are you ever accused of being fickle? Do you change your mind about as often as you change your panties? Don't sweat it! *Fickle* is just a not-so-nice word for *flexible*. People who can't be flexible get stuck in ruts instead of having the guts to recognize that they may have made a wrong choice. When you're flexible, you're not afraid to say, "I chose that once, but now I'm choosing something different."

74. Are your legs sore from a marathon hike through the mall? Bend over at your waist and bend your knees a little. Then slowly "walk" down your legs with your hands. Rest your hands on the floor (or as close as you can get to it) and stay like that for as long as it feels good. Feel the big muscles in your back and the back of your legs loosen and relax.

75. Looking for a new way to share fun with your best gal-pals? Have a beauty blast! Make up cute le invitations for a Spa Night at your place and give them to our friends. Tell everyone to bring their fave beauty care cts to share. Make sure that stuff for facials, manicures, es, and hair care are included. Leave a big basket by the re each spa customer can contribute her offering.

Then pop up some popcorn,
crank up some girly tunes,
and let the beautifying begin!

TRY THIS!

When you're hungry but
don't want to grab greasy chips or
junk food, whip up a smoothie. Toss one
banana, ½ cup strawberries, and ½ cup low-fat
milk or vanilla yogurt in the blender. Voilà—a
delicious batch of healthy smoothies for you and
your friends! Next time, experiment with different
fruits and foods to go with the milk or yogurt,
like banana and peanut butter, or peaches
and honey. Get creative and invent your own
signature smoothie!

76 Want to incorporate more exercise into your daily life?
Go out for a team sport! Those daily practice
sessions will keep you in top form, and you'll make new pals and
learn new skills at the same time. If you're not the sporty type but
more of a romantic, sign up for dance lessons. Some communities
even offer free classes in retro-chic dances like the mambo, cha-cha,
and the waltz.

77 Are you sick of everyone being on your back about grades?
Think about it for a minute. Could it be that the people
who are bugging you most about your schoolwork are doing it
because they care about you? Why else would it matter to anyone
what your report card looks like? Your education won't make or
break THEIR lives, but it could make or break YOURS! Here's a

secret: The kids who do the best in school aren't necessarily the smartest ones—but they *are* the wisest because they've figured out that getting good grades *now* makes a lot of things easier down the road. All you need to do to get kickin grades is to want to badly enough, so make the effort!

CATCH THE BUZZ!

Actress Rene Russo says, "Wisdom is better than rubies or pearls or anything you could wish for."

78 Rumors are the worst. If you're ever tempted to spread a nasty rumor, imagine how you would feel if it was being spread about you! Very few rumors you hear are entirely true anyway. They usually start with a grain of truth that gets cruddier and cruddier the more it spreads. Why? Most often the spreaders are jealous of or angry at the person the rumor is about. They use lies or half-lies to trash someone behind her back because they don't have the guts to square off with her face-to-face. Let people know you're not into gossip by showing concern for the one being gossiped about. Your lab partner says, "Did you hear what Katy did in gym? She totally spazzed out on the b-ball court and tried to shoot at the wrong basket. What a moron!" And you say, "Katy's so brainy at math. I think I'll offer to give her a few basketball tips in exchange for some homework help. Thanks for the great idea!" You've let your lab partner know you're not into gossip without coming right out and telling her she's a twit for spreading it.

79 Looking to earn some extra cash? Start a baby-sitting or pet-care business. It's a big commitment, but if you're responsible, you can make it a real success have a blast, too.

Question! I would love to get a baby-sitting business going. How do I get started?

Answer! First, take a CPR class if you can find one. Many hospitals offer them, and some offer general baby-sitting courses, too. (If you plan to baby-sit infants, you'll have to take a special class for infant CPR.) Then make a list of all your prior baby-sitting experience. Call the parents of the kids you've sat for before and ask them if they'd mind if you listed them as references for your future clients. While you have them on the phone, ask them to spread the word to their friends that you are looking for more baby-sitting work. Make your reference list (a list of the people you've sat for before with their phone numbers) as neat as you can and make plenty of copies. The best way to drum up business is to network, and that means telling everyone you know about your new business plans. When you hear about a potential new client, ask if you can meet with her at her convenience and tell her what makes you a good baby-sitter. Tell her about any CPR or child-care classes you've taken, offer her a copy of your reference list, and let her see how you interact with her kids. Soon you'll be booked solid!

Q
u
i
&
c
K
i
A
E

80 Competition is a part of life, even among friends. And a little competition can be healthy, especially in sports. But **when competition turns to catfights, take a step back and examine the friendship.** Whatever it is you're feeling ultracompetitive about—popularity, academic achievement, physical achievement, or even romance—chances are, you're not seeing the situation clearly. Most competitive feelings come from a belief that there is a limited

supply of something. Try to visualize that SOMETHING as a limit-less resource. There's plenty of it to go around, so be happy about sharing it with your friends! For example, if one pal gets an A on a test, that doesn't mean that there's one less A for you. If your bud has a boyfriend and you don't, be happy for her! Your chances of finding the right boy for you aren't hurt by your friend having found one first.

81 Divorce is one of the hardest things a kid can go through. It's normal to be sad, confused, or angry. But don't let yourself feel guilty about your parents' divorce. As much as it might feel otherwise, the problem is between your parents, and you are in no way the cause of it. Even if you are mad at your mom or dad, try to talk about your feelings with them. They both love you and want what's best for you. Remember that they're both going through some pretty rough emotions themselves and each of them could use a friend. It can feel like the end of the world when your family breaks apart; but if you look around, you can probably find some of your friends who have lived through it and are enjoying happy relationships with each of their parents. Picturing yourself in a similar situation down the road may help you to get through the stressful days ahead. If talking to your parents or other family members doesn't help, go see your school counselor. Sometimes the best person to talk to someone who's not already involved.

TRY THIS!

Have you heard of support groups? Adults have support groups for just about every adult problem there is, so why shouldn't kids have them, too? If you're stressing about your parents' divorce, make a list of the kids you know who've been there or are going through the same thing. Invite them all to meet at your house one day to compare notes. Sometimes hearing other people's stories can really put your own problems into perspective.

82 So your older sister just got a bikini and she actually fills it out. You're thinking that both of your breasts together couldn't fill *one* of her cups. You begin formulating a secret plot to "accidentally" wash her bikini in hot water along with all of her bras, then throw them all in the dryer on High so that by the time you're done, they might fit your old Barbies. Wait a minute! Before you turn demolition-demon, take a look in the mirror. Repeat these words: "I am beautiful just the way I am." Now do it without cracking up. Do it over and over and over again until you don't feel silly doing it! Your breasts will continue developing until you're about 18, and anyway, bigger is not always better! For all you know, YOU are the envy of those big-chested girls in your school who hide their curves under oversized sweaters and have to wear uncomfortable sports bras every time they exercise. Love what you've got!

83 Who loves you with complete devotion absolutely all the time, no matter what? Your pet! Show your four-legged pal your appreciation by finding fun stuff to do with him! Dogs need exercise, so take Fifi to the park and teach her Frisbee. Play bowling with your cat: Get a big yarn ball and some dominoes and see who wins. Be creatively silly and come up with exciting activities for your bird, iguana, or rabbit. The little guys depend on you for fun, so don't let them down!

84 What's going on in your school or community? Are things fair and as they should be, or is there some injustice that really got you bugged? If you don't like something, stop feeling

TRY THIS! Join student government in your school. Get active in determining the policies and politics you have to live by—find your VOICE!

powerless about it. Everyone has the ability to effect change. If you're sure that your position is one of fairness and justice, fight for what's right!

85 Are the friends you enjoy the most today the same ones you enjoyed the most last year? You'll find that a lot of your true friendships will last throughout your school years (and some may last your whole lifetime), but there will be others that will come to an end. It's never easy to part ways with someone who has been very special to you. Maybe you feel guilty over being the one who decided to move on, or maybe you feel hurt at being left behind. The truth is that people change, sometimes slowly and sometimes practically overnight. When one person in a friendship becomes a different person, she'll naturally want to be around people who are more like the new her. Try to be gentle when leaving old relationships behind. Remember how much you and your friend shared and be glad for the good memories. You may find you enjoy your new batch of buds a zillion times more right now, but who knows? You and your old pal might hook up again in the future when you're both back on the same wavelength.

86 Almost everyone feels shy at one time or another. But for some people, shyness becomes a real problem that keeps them from enjoying life as much as they could. If you are suffering from shyness, ask yourself what makes you afraid to be more social. Is it a fear of rejection? Try taking one very small risk, like asking someone you don't know very well a question about a class you have together. You may find that t's easier than you thought it would be. The next day, try pushing urself a little harder and share a joke with someone you're feeling imidated by. Every day, make a point of reaching out more and e to people. Don't wait for people to be friendly to you; introduce

TRY THIS!

yourself to new kids and be friendly first. Soon you may find yourself saying to your friends, "You won't believe this, but I used to be shy."

Join a club or team at school, or sign up for an extracurricular class that interests you like art, dancing, or photography. Sharing interests with other kids as well as getting out and doing new things with new people may help you to overcome the shyness bug.

87 Feeling bored is a huge waste of time! If you're stuck indoors, you could: redecorate your room, plan your wardrobe for the next week, organize all those loose photographs into a scrapbook, get artsy with some paint or clay, make a "cheer up" card for a friend or relative who's feeling down, or play your favorite music and practice your dance moves in front of the mirror! And if the weather's nice, you have even less of an excuse for being bored! Get your bored little behind outside and go roller blading or bike riding. Even a walk around the block will boost your energy level. Enjoy your own company or hook up with some pals. Just don't sit around like a couch potato or *you'll* be the one who's boring.

TRY THIS!

Paint-it-yourself ceramic studios are popping up all over the place; maybe there's one where you live. (Look in your yellow pages under Ceramics, Pottery, or Clay Products.) At most of them, you pick out some little plate, cup, bowl, dish, picture frame, or other piece of pottery that's already made, and paint it any cute and funky way you want. The place fires your piece for you and you can pick it up in about a week. It's really fun!

88 Put your best face forward! The key to tak good care of your face is to know your skin type. If y have dry and flaky skin, wash with a very gentle cleanser and experiment with different moisturizers to see which one works best for you. If your skin is oily, you may need to wash twice a day and use a toner or astringent. Either way, be gentle! The more you tug and scrub on your delicate facial skin, the worse it will look. Drinking lots of water and getting plenty of rest may be the best skin-care tricks of all.

TRY THIS!

If your oily skin has a tendency to look really shiny, try powder leaves. They're thin sheets of paper with a light coating of powder that absorbs oil. You can find them in most drugstores, and they come in little pads that are tiny enough to slip right in your pocket—you just tear one out whenever you need it. They're much better than powder makeup that can leave you looking like a pancake-face!

89 Body hairs can pop up in the weirdest places—sometimes even around your nipples. Don't wig out if you sprout a few booby-hairs! There's no need to shave 'em, pluck 'em, or wax 'em. Leave the little buggers alone; they're completely normal and natural.

90 Everyone needs to set aside a few minutes each day to be alone with her thoughts—a chance to look inside and get in touch with her deepest, wisest, truest self. You can call it meditation, prayer, or plain old alone-time—just do it! One way to remind yourself to keep up this habit is to set up a special spot in your room for it. You could create your sacred space around a ight table, windowsill, or even a ⸳rdboard box. To decorate your ⸳ed space, gather up all the ⸳ts that make you feel really ⸳-pictures of family members, ⸳ other loved ones, maybe a

stuffed teddy you've had since childhood, a small vase for real flowers you can pick from the backyard, a small mirror to help you find the real you, a pretty rock, crystal, or leaf—something to symbolize the natural world—and maybe some potpourri in your favorite fragrance. Once you have your sacred space just the way you want it, sit comfortably before it and try to block all stressful thoughts out of your mind. Let yourself just be, or focus on happy things. You will come to love this special place and the special times you carve out just for you!

91 **Going bra shopping can be exciting, embarrassing, and confusing, so don't go it alone!** Take your mom, older sister, aunt, or someone else you trust and love. The sales clerk will measure you and bring you different selections in your size. If none of them feels comfortable, speak up! Don't be afraid to suggest that the sales clerk might have made a mistake in determining your size. Politely ask her to measure you again, and don't leave with anything that doesn't feel 100 percent comfortable. Make sure that you can easily fasten and unfasten each bra yourself, and stick to neutral colors so that you won't have to worry about anyone seeing your bright red bra through your thin white shirt!

92 No two breasts are exactly alike—not even the two on your body. It's completely normal for your breasts to be two different sizes, even as much as a cup size different. **Don't freak over a mismatched pair!** No one except you will ever notice the difference.

93 Don't you just hate know-it-alls? They're the people who don't listen to a word you're saying because they're too busy planning in their heads what they're going to say next. Listening is one of the best habits there is, so **try to be a good listener.** It will make you smart, it will make you popu and you'll get to find out about a lot of cool stuff!

94 **Be kind to your hair!** Healthy hair is beautiful hair, and hair usually is its healthiest when you let it do its own thing. That means if it's curly, make the most of the curls; if it's straight, wear it stylishly straight; and whatever color it is—let the true beauty of its natural color shine through! Curling irons, straightening irons, and any kind of chemical processing all damage hair and make it break and split unevenly. Everyone wants to look her best, but don't make the mistake of assuming that your best is anything different from what you naturally are. You'll look totally beauteous if you make the most of your hair by giving it plenty of TLC. Be gentle when brushing out tangles (use a comb, never a brush!), and take it easy with the blow-dryer. Never blow-dry your hair on the hottest setting.

TRY THIS!

If you're looking for fullness, try bending over at the waist and gently blow-drying your hair at the roots only. Flip your head back up, run your fingers through your hair, and let the ends dry naturally.

95 Do you rate your folks as way-cool or way-strict? Their rules for you may have more to do with YOU than them. You figure you're older so you want more freedom now, right? Well, in the eyes of your parents, more freedom comes not with age but with responsibility. You've got to give to get. If you want your parents to recognize that you're growing up, show them that you are by taking on more responsibility around the house. Live by their rules without any complaints slipups for a while before you try to convince them to change the s. They'll probably give you more freedom when you start show-em how well you can handle it.

Question! Help! My mother makes me call her from everywhere I go. I have to give her the telephone number of places where there are parties and all of my friends' houses. Why doesn't she trust me?

Answer! Who says she doesn't trust you? If she truly didn't, she wouldn't let you go to parties and your friends' houses in the first place. She's really not asking so much by just wanting to know where you are. What if she needed to get in touch with you because of some emergency? Aren't you glad you know where to get in touch with her in case anything comes up that causes you to really need her?

96 Do you think you're ready for makeup, but your parents don't agree? **Try wearing just lip gloss and a little sheer mascara.** If they see you're aiming to meet them halfway, maybe they'll be cool with it. Besides, less is more—look in any fashion magazine! You don't want to cover up your beauty—let it shine!

97 Do you ever feel like no one listens to you? **Try listening to yourself.** If you think your parents are being unfair about something, say everything that's on your mind out loud, by yourself, pretending that they are sitting right next to you. This will give you a chance to listen to what you're saying and be sure it makes good sense before your parents hear it.

TRY THIS!

Having an imaginary conversation with someone also works well when you need to talk about something that's hard or embarrassing. Pretend the pers you need to talk to is sitting a chair across from you, and all your feelings out—it wi make having the real conver much easier and less scary

98 So, you've got an occasion coming up where you need to get totally decked out. You're psyched to wear the dress, but the thought of the shoes makes your feet hurt already. **Stick a couple of Band-Aids on each heel and a little one on each pinky toe.** Make sure your shoes cover the Band-Aids, or experiment with clear Band-Aids if you're wearing regular stockings. (If you're wearing black tights, no sweat!) Your feet will thank you later!

99 OK, you've met this guy and you think that he is the greatest thing ever (you've even taken your #1 poster-boy off the wall). There's nothing wrong with being excited about meeting someone who seems fantastic, but **give it around a month before you decide that you're crazy about him.** No matter how cute he is and how nice he seems today, there's no way you can really get to know someone in less time than that. Smart girls take a while before they give their hearts away!

100 Do you or any of your friends have a video camera lying around the house? Ask a parent if you can borrow it. (Get a quick lesson if you haven't used it before!) Then **make a movie starring you and your best buds!** Wear your fave duds and interview one another about the things that ~~a~~re important to you. Sing a few bars ~~of~~ the most right-now song. Think ~~how~~ much fun it will be to watch it when you're all graduating high ~~schoo~~l, again when you're graduating college . . . and maybe even ~~one d~~ay when you're having a bridal shower for the first one of you ~~going~~ down the aisle!

101 **Conquer your fears!** The only way to get over feeling afraid of something is to do it! Fear is a fact of life, but that doesn't mean you can't push past it. Maybe you're afraid of talking to kids you don't know very well. Maybe you're afraid to try out for a team. Maybe you're afraid to stand up to a cousin who's treating you badly. Whatever your fear, the key to overcoming it is to realize that EVERYONE has fears just like yours. Accept your fear, face it head-on, and just do whatever it is you're afraid of. You'll feel great afterward!

102 Make a difference! **Volunteer!** We know you've probably got a gazillion demands on your time, but if you can spare just one afternoon a month, find a local cause you believe in and commit yourself to a selfless act. You won't believe how fab it can make you feel. Maybe there's a nursing home nearby full of lonely people who could use some conversation, or a park that needs cleaning up, or an organization that collects food and clothing for those who can't afford it. Ask an adult to help you research the possibilities. You won't regret it!

CATCH THE BUZZ!
Author Henry David Thoreau said, "It isn't enough to be busy. Ants are busy. The question is: What are we busy about?"

103 Ever feel like you're stuck in a monotonous routine? Sometimes you need to do something different to change your perspective a little and get yourself out of a rut. One beautiful and simple remedy for the bored-with-life blues is to set your clock extra-early one morning and actually **go outside and watch the sun rise.** You'll be surprised by how pretty it is and how peaceful and thankful it can make you feel.

104 Sure, those hip-hugging bell-bottoms look great on some people (like walking pretzel sticks) but not on all of us. Don't be a fashion slave. Just because a magazine says it's hip doesn't mean it will work for everyone's body type. Fashion designers say the key to looking great is to play up your best features. **Experiment with different styles to see which ones really work for YOU.** Do you like the way you look in long, flowing dresses, or do flirty little skirts and tees better flatter your body type? The secret to putting together great outfits is to keep PROPORTION in mind. That means if you're wearing baggy jeans, wear a close-fitting top. If you're wearing a big, loose sweater, pair it with close-fitting pants or a straight skirt. Let your imagination run wild! No one else has your particular, individual taste, so dress in what makes *you* feel comfortable. Be your own original!

CATCH THE BUZZ!

When it comes to fashion, actress Geena Davis says, "My rule is that there aren't any rules."

105 When someone asks, "Can you keep a secret?" do you swear that you can but then have a hard time doing it? **When you're tempted to pass on a juicy whopper someone has entrusted you with, think about how you would feel if that person betrayed your confidence.** Secrets deserve to be kept! (There is one exception, though. If you hear a secret about someone who is being hurt or in serious trouble, you owe it to that person to share the secret with a caring adult who can help.)

106 Do you know any kids who drink or do drugs? Do you think they're happy? Maybe you've seen kids drinking or ˙ng drugs who look like they're having the time of their lives. Did ever see them the next morning? They're sick and miserable.

Drinking alcohol and doing drugs make people act differently than they normally would. Knowing who you are and being in control of your actions will give you the best shot at making your teenage years an outrageous funfest. But every time someone takes drugs or takes a drink, she gives up that chance for a really cool experience by giving up control of herself. If you ever worry about being embarrassed in regular situations, just think about how easy it is to do stuff you'll be majorly embarrassed by or regret when you don't even have control over your actions! Drinking and taking drugs is not only stupid, it's illegal and incredibly dangerous. Kids who do it don't like themselves. They think it will make them seem more mature and grown-up, but all they're doing is copying the worst of the grown-up population! More and more teens are deciding that the coolest way to be mature is to be healthy and clearheaded about their choices and their fun. Join the new wave and be proud to JUST SAY NO.

107 It's a proven fact that the earlier a person begins drinking, the more likely it is that she will become an alcoholic. The National Institute on Alcohol Abuse and Alcoholism studied 42,000 people and found that 43 percent of kids who take their first drink before starting high school become alcoholics. Have you ever known an alcoholic? Alcoholism is one of the most horrible conditions a person could ever have to deal with. If you don't drink until after the age of 21, your chances of becoming an alcoholic go down to 10 percent. Kids who drink are taking a big risk that they'll seriously mess up their lives . . . and for what? The chance to show off to some other kids who are already messing up big time? Be the strong one. Be true to YOU. Don't drink.

108 Smiling releases happy waves in our brains (scientists call them endorphins). So when you're in a funk, try smiling for no reason and hook up to your own *natural* high. Laugh out loud, or sing. People may think you're nuts, b· so what?

109 The best defense against a bully? CONFIDENCE! Once you show a bully that you're not going to let him or her bother you, you may find that you're no longer a victim. Bullies lack confidence in themselves, and pushing other people around makes them feel more important. If you make sure bullies know you aren't the least bit rattled by them, it won't be fun for them to pick on you anymore.

CATCH THE BUZZ!

Actress Jennifer Love Hewitt says, "Standing up for myself and deciding to be my own person was the smartest thing I did growing up."

110 Pimples got you popping mad? Relax! Stressing out over your complexion is a proven way to make it worse. It probably doesn't comfort you at all to know that most young people get some acne at least some of the time, but it's true! About all you can do is make sure to wash your face morning and night with a gentle cleanser, get plenty of rest, eat lots of fresh, healthy foods, and keep your fingers crossed!

Q & A **QUIZ TIME**

Question! Sometimes at night I go to bed without taking off my makeup and washing my face. My skin looks fine, so is it OK to do this?

Answer! No way! Your skin might look good right now, but bacteria and dirt could be clogging your pores. That means the next time you're stressed, you may have a major breakout. So wash up!

11 When you judge someone by the way he or she looks, you're stereotyping that person. It's dumb and unfair. Get to someone before you form an opinion about

him or her. Try to imagine how you would feel if someone automatically didn't like you because of your brown hair or blue eyes.

112. Do you ever feel caught between being a kid and an adult? Most girls your age feel this way. A lot of adult responsibilities are being laid on you, but you still don't have the opportunities and choices of real adulthood. It can feel unfair at times, but try to keep in mind that you're still getting some of the perks of being a kid, too, like not having to worry about paying for your home, food, and most of your clothes! Look for things to appreciate about this in-the-middle time, and you'll see that being your age has a lot of advantages!

TRY THIS!

When you're feeling pulled in a million impossible directions, try this relaxation technique: Lie down or sit comfortably and close your eyes. Pretend you're a firmly packed snowman. In your mind, picture your head, arms, legs, and body. Now imagine that the sun is rising over you. It feels wonderful. It's so comforting as it slowly warms your body. The sun gets hotter, and inch by inch you feel your feet beginning to melt. The heat travels up your legs, and slowly the rest of you melts, piece by piece. Do this so that your whole body melts and feels warm and relaxed.

113 **Stick to your principles!** If all your friends wanted to play a trick on someone they had decided was unpopular, would you go along or would you do what you feel in your heart is right? Everybody wants to be accepted, but you have to make sure the crowd you're looking for acceptance from is up to *your* standards.

CATCH THE BUZZ!

Princess Diana said, "I am going to own myself and be true to myself. I no longer want to live someone else's idea of what and who I should be."

114 When you were little, did anyone ever tell you that nice girls don't get angry? Did perfect strangers ever ask, "Why aren't you smiling, honey?" Our society expects cheerfulness and sweetness from girls, but let's face it—girls don't always feel all that sugary! **When you notice yourself pasting on a fake smile to cover up some negative emotion you're feeling, stop!** You have the right to feel gnarly sometimes.

115 Did you ever notice how people who are nice become better looking the more you get to know them? One of the best beauty secrets has nothing to do with your face, hair, or figure. It's a proven fact that people who are warm, open, and honest are rated as more attractive than people who shallow and superficial.

TRY THIS!

Your mom yelled at you this morning, your teacher gave you a C on your science test, and you're feeling angry at the world. Go home and punch something. Punch a pillow or a cushion, or get some clay and really smash it. These are great ways of getting out your frustrations on *something* rather than *someone*.

Stop worrying so much about your exterior polish up what's inside!

CATCH THE BUZZ!

Actress Alicia Silverstone says, "My secret to style is being a good person. I like being kind, considerate, and compassionate . . . That's the most beautiful thing you can be."

116 We all need sunshine. It keeps you healthy and can even improve your mood! So when the blues hit, run outside for a quick boost—just don't forget your sunscreen!

117 No matter how annoying your younger brothers or sisters can be, try to give your sibs a break now and then. You've got to admit it's cool how much they look up to you. If you're always telling them to get lost, you might lose out on teaching them all the lessons you've learned so far.

118 Have you had your first-ever visit from the period fairy yet? If you haven't, don't take it personally. She isn't avoiding you for any particular reason. Most girls start menstruating when they're 11 or 12, but it's perfectly normal to start as early as 9 or as late as 16. For some girls, it's a huge emotional deal—the sign of real womanhood, and for others it's just no biggie. Don't expect to feel much of anything when it happens. The only side effects you might notice are tummy cramps, tender breasts, bloating, lower back pain, pimples, or feeling pooped, but none of these will be dramatic enough to give you a real heads up. You'll just know you got it when you see it.

119 Are you freaked by the prospect of a period debut for which you're unprepared? Lots of girls worry about a mega-embarrassing public display, but it rarely happens. Your flow will probably be pretty light at first, and you'll have time to get supplie before it gets out of hand. It's not a bad idea to buy some pac and inspect the things before you need them so you're r perplexed when the moment comes. Then tuck a few in your locker, along with a sweater to tie around your waist just in case the worst happens. (You can always offer your stash to a friend in need, and she'll be forever appreciative of your preparedness and generosity.) If you are caught at school without supplies, go directly to the nurse's office. Don't be embarrassed—it won't be the first time she's had a visit like that. She'll help you out, and if your clothes *have* gotten stained, you can hang with her until your mom brings a change. After that first initiation into womanhood, you can expect your period to come every 28 days or so. Some girls are super-regular, and others could be off by as much as a week or more. When you first start getting it, you may even skip a month here and there—nothing to freak over.

120 Some lucky chicas breeze through p-time barely noticing it, while others get hit with cramps, fatigue, and a general yuck feeling. If you're in this second group, experiment to see what makes you feel better. Take a walk or a jog outside. Dance around the living room while you watch videos. Anything that gets your body moving may help ease cramps and crankiness. If exercise doesn't right you, take some pain medication and a nap. Some girls swear by warm milk or herbal teas. Sometimes a warm bath or a heating pad on your tummy works.

121 If you've never used a tampon, the very concept may sound as terrifying and improbable to you as walking around with a carrot up your nose. But they're really not as gross as they sound. Most girls will start out with pads, and some women go through their whole lives using just pads. If you're happy with pads and have no desire to shake up your monthly routine, no prob. Don't let friends or ads put any pressure on you to do anything you have no desire to do. But if you're curious, read the directions that come in any box of tampons and give it a whirl. You may want to lay a hand mirror on the floor so you can see what you're doing better. The best success tip: RELAX. If you hurt anywhere, you're not positioning the thing correctly. You shouldn't feel tampons at all once they're in place, and they can be pretty handy for swim days and heavy-flow times. Just memorize the package directions and don't forget to change plugs frequently!

122 Do you ever wish your parents were a little *more* involved in your life? (If you're rolling on the floor convulsed with laughter right now, skip to the next tip—this one obviously isn't for you.) Seriously, while most girls feel their parents' interest in their doings is far too intense, there are some who get total freedom from their folks—and hate it. Adding new, adultlike activities to your life can be scary and sometimes disastrous without the guidance of, well . . . an *adult*, who's been there before. If your parents say stuff like "We know you can handle it" about things you're pretty sure you can't handle, sit them down for a chat. They might have had extra-strict parents themselves and sworn that they'd let *their* kids find their own way. They might think they're doing you a favor. Gently tell your folks that you appreciate their trust in you, but you'd love to hear their opinions about the stuff you're doing or planning to do. They'll probably be flattered! Just like there are some parents who try to keep their daughters in childhood too long, there are others who try to rush them into adulthood too fast. If your folks are so psyched about their little girl becoming a woman that they pressure you to dress or act in a way that's more mature than you're feeling inside, talk to them. Thank them for their support, but tell them that you're going to be a grown-up for a long, long time and you don't have much time left to enjoy the advantages of being a kid.

123 When fall rolls around, do you always find yourself pining for some of those fab new fashions? If you've found a way to snag a few bucks over the summer, stash a portion of your pay each week in an envelope marked "fall." (But you can't dip into it every time you're short!) You could have a big chunk saved by September—maybe enough for an entire too-cute, first-day-of-school outfit!

124 **Ignore anyone who says things like "Don't be a crybaby."** Being able to cry is a sign that you express your emotions easily. Holding in your feelings doesn't make them go away—it just makes you sick!

125 Surfin' the Net can be FUN (and educational) but **be careful in chat rooms.** You never know what kind of people you're going to meet there. If a stranger wants to get your E-mail address or telephone number, tell him you'll meet him in cyberspace but your real identity is classified info!

126 If you want your nails to grow, **don't mess with your cuticles.** Cuticles are those little pieces of skin that grow all around where your nails meet your fingers. Never bite or pull them. It could lead to an infection and, besides, it really hurts. To get your nails in tip-top shape, try rubbing a good lotion on your cuticles every night.

TRY THIS!
Keep your nail polish fresh by storing it in the fridge. It feels great in the summer and your manicure will last a lot longer.

127 At some point in our lives, we all feel lonely. When you're feeling lonely and depressed, maybe you're wishing you had a boyfriend, a better body, or that you were smarter or more talented. These are the kinds of self-defeating thoughts that keep people feeling bad! The big secret is: No one can make you happy except yourself. You have the power to do ANYTHING and that includes changing your life for the better. **If you don't like something about yourself or your life, start making changes,** step-by-step, every day. And don't give up!

CATCH THE BUZZ!
Actress Jada Pinkett Smith says, "I think the smartest thing any woman can do is take control of her life!"

128 If you have lost someone you love, the best thing you can do is reach out. This is the time to surround yourself with the ones who care about you. It's what family and friends are for! You may not feel like talking right away and that's fine. But don't shut out the people who love you right at the time when you need them the most.

129 Has anyone ever told you that you're too sensitive? It hurts when people don't want to acknowledge your feelings. People your age feel things strongly, and that's OK! The next time you are accused of being too sensitive, ask the other person how she'd feel in your shoes. Maybe she truly wouldn't react as strongly as you, but that is just a difference in personality types and it doesn't mean there's anything wrong with you for feeling the way you do.

Q & A

Question! I baby-sit for a really nice family. The problem is that the father sometimes makes rude remarks to me about the way I dress or look. He does this in a joking way, but it really hurts my feelings. What should I do?

Answer! If he is making comments that you think are out of line or degrading, you should speak up. You don't ever have to put up with being harassed by people, no matter who they are. Depending on the severity of his comments, decide if you can talk to him or if you should go right to your parents. Don't let this continue!

130 SMART GIRLS RULE! Nothing is more attractive than a smart woman, so ditch the cute sweet-and-simple image! Read about things that interest you and listen to everything around you. If the guy's worth impressing, he's worth impressing with your brains.

131 The phrase "I promise!" is sometimes taken lightly, but true buds know that those two words mean a lot. Before you blow off a commitment to someone you care about, imagine the hurt look on her face as she cries, "But you promised!"

132 Right now it's probably pretty easy to get mad at your mom for dumb things or to be embarrassed by her. But try not to shut your mom out! Chances are good that she loves you more than anyone else in the world even if she does drive you nutty sometimes. Your relationship with your mom is a different one now that you're less dependent on her. (And it will still change a few more times as you get older.) It takes effort to keep an ever-changing relationship strong and happy, so why don't you make the first move? After all, YOU'RE the one who's been doing all the changing—she's pretty much the same mom you've always had. Get to know her. One of the neat things about mothers and daughters is that eventually they're both adult women who can be real friends to one another. As you grow, your mom will let you see more and more of the whole woman she is (instead of just letting you see her mom side). If you show her that you're ready for it, she may start treating you as more of an equal. And even if she's not always cool, she'll always be a part of your life and she'll probably always be the one person who will stick up for you when no one else will. Suggest sometimes that just the two of you go out for a meal, a walk, or to the movies.

133 We all need water, but very few of us drink enough. Water helps our bodies work, it helps our skin look good, and it keeps us from being bloated. So bring that water bottle with you everywhere!

134 Do you ever feel like you don't know who you really are? You're not your name, your sex, your nationality, or your street address. The person you are has been there all along, but sometimes it seems like you're inventing yourself every day. The best way to stay true to yourself is to pay attention to your feelings. Keep a journal and write down how you feel about everything in your life! There's no reason to write anything but the absolute truth, since no one will ever read it but you. With so many outside influences, the real you can get lost if you don't make a point of keeping YOU in sight.

Quick **Q & A**

Question! Some kids I know are already thinking about college and careers, but I have no idea what I want to do. I'm not especially good at anything and I don't have any real passions that I know of. How do I decide?

Answer! You're way ahead of yourself! Kids who are making those decisions now are likely to change their minds a couple of times before they find the careers that are right for them. You'll have plenty of time to think about what you'd like to do before you start college, and even then you won't have to pick a major your first year. You may not find what interests you most until you get there.

135 If you're really curious now about what kind of career might be best for you, try this exercise: Write down five places you've enjoyed visiting on your own and five places you'd love to visit if you had all the money and time you needed. Why did you choose those places? How did they make you feel? Imagine yourself in each place and look around. Who's working there? Is it a job you can see yourself doing? Think about all the different careers that could relate to these places and picture yourself in each of them. For instance, if you love hiking or visiting a park, you might enjoy becoming a forest ranger or working out-

doors or with animals. If you get excited about spending time at museums, you could become a docent, artist, archivist, archaeologist, or paleontologist. If the library's your thing, you could be a writer, illustrator, or librarian. Remember that ANY career is within your reach if you have a true passion for it!

136 Your honest opinion is important and you probably feel flattered when someone asks for it. But sometimes "brutal honesty" is just that—brutal. If your honest opinion would wound or put down another person, think twice about how you give it!

137 Don't you love being around someone with a great sense of humor? Genuine belly laughs that you share with someone else are certain to make you feel closer to that person. But humor is hard to define and what's funny to one person may not be funny to the next. Sometimes it's tempting to fake a laugh to try to get someone to like you, or to stifle your own laughter if you don't think others will share it. Don't do it—be true to your own individual sense of humor! You'll get more enjoyment out of your experiences that way, and you'll tune in better to the buds who are right for you.

138 Ever wonder how those girls in magazines and on TV always have perfect complexions? They don't! In the worlds of fashion modeling and acting, experts are on hand to make sure every zit becomes completely invisible before the camera starts rolling. In real life, real girls get acne and that includes famous ones! Don't pick, pop, or squeeze your zits. You may get momentary satisfaction, but you could also end up with scars or pimples that linger for weeks. Your best weapon against acne is a defensive strategy. Eat well, sleep well, and wash well. Steer clear of moisturizers, makeup, and sunscreens that contain oil. Look for products labeled "non-comedogenic," since they won't clog your pores.

139 "You can't do this, and you can't do that either." Sometimes it seems like life is too full of rules. It can drive you practically postal, but the fact is that most of these rules really are in place for good reasons. The ability to follow rules is a sign of a mature person. You may think that once you're older you won't have to live by so many rules, but guess what! The rules never end. When you drive, you have to follow traffic rules. When you work, you have to follow the rules of the company that hired you. And you'll always have to honor the law (the rules of our country). The thing to remember about rules is that you usually get something good in return for obeying them. Think about the rules at a movie theater—no talking, no throwing candy, no blading up and down the aisles. But in exchange for following those rules, you get to see the movie!

140 When you get angry or upset, you probably think that someone or something made you feel that way. But the truth is that nothing outside of you has any real power to make you happy or sad! If someone makes fun of the new boots you love, it's up to you to decide how you feel about them. You could choose to let that person's opinion bum you out or you could choose to laugh it off and feel great about your own individual sense of style.

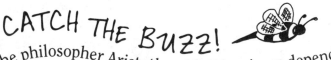

CATCH THE BUZZ!
The philosopher Aristotle said, "Happiness depends upon ourselves."

141 If you're getting really ticked off at your older sister because she always has advice for you on this or that, chill out. Annoying as she is, she might be right! Take advantage of her having done things a few paces ahead of you. You might get to sidestep some mistakes and embarrassing moments from hearing about her escapades.

142 So you stayed up late watching the MTV Video Music Awards and woke up with your face looking totally tired and puffy. Fill a big bowl with ice water, take a deep breath, and dunk your face right in there. It sounds like torture, but it really works to reduce the swelling, and you wanted some help waking up anyway, right?

143 Is cleaning your room on your list of top-10 yuck-chores, while getting it messy seems unavoidable? Maybe you're the type who has to try on a couple of outfits before school every day until you find the right one. But letting all those clothes accumulate until the weekend means spending a whole afternoon indoors picking up. Try making a promise to yourself that you won't get into bed at night until you've hung up all the clothes you tried on or wore that day. Then plan a weekend that ROCKS!

144 It's not something you probably think about much, but every one of us has a *comfort zone*. Your comfort zone determines the limitations you put upon yourself. It is working *for* you when it keeps you from taking unnecessary risks or allowing yourself to be talked into things that you know you'd later regret, like drinking or smoking. But your comfort zone can work *against* you in other areas. Do you long to meet new people but feel more comfortable just sticking with your established friends? Do you feel your baby-sitting services are worth a few bucks more than you're charging, but you're not comfortable raising your price? Do you fantasize about bringing home a straight-A report card but feel comfortable with your Bs? Try being aware of your comfort zone and widening it by just a little bit every week. Take a tiny risk. Talk to someone you didn't think you had the guts to start a conversation with. Go see a teacher about a grade you feel is unfair. Join a club that none of your friends would join. If you make sure every risk you take has integrity and love behind it (for yourself and for others), you'll build confidence and a richer life for yourself. It feels awesome to watch your comfort zone get bigger and bigger!

145 Buy a big wall calendar you love.

Scribbling all your practices, meetings, and plans in the squares is fun and it's a great way to make sure you don't forget anything or double-book yourself. Plus, when you're feeling blue, one look at your calendar will remind you of all the cool stuff you have going on!

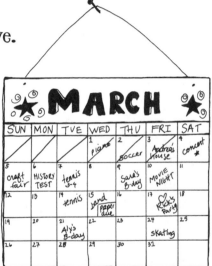

146

What do you remember being praised for most when you were a little girl? Do lines like "What a pretty dress!" or "Look what beautiful eyes she has!" or "Your hair is lovely in that style" sound familiar? It's sad that girls are most often praised for their looks while boys are praised for their accomplishments. Which kind of praise do you think is better for the self-esteem of a growing child? If you're still judging your own worth by how you look, you gotta break out of that pattern! Make a list of all the great things you say, feel, dream, think, and do—THAT is who you are, no matter what your outer covering looks like.

147 **Stick up for the underdog!** When someone is being teased or unfairly criticized, show your strength of character by defending him or her. It's always easiest to jump in and agree with the group, but if that means attacking someone who doesn't deserve it, you'll be glad in the long run that you were strong enough to go against the crowd.

CATCH THE BUZZ!

Actress Jenna Elfman says, "Try not to care too much what other people think."

148 Wondering why NONE of the guys in your grade comes even close to being as to-die-for as your fave actors and musicians? First of all, remember that those ultra-cuties are hand-picked from thousands of regular guys for the specific purpose of making your heart race. And, secondly, **give the guys in your class some time!** They'll probably improve a lot over the next few years. Even that babe on the cover of your newest teen mag was probably a dork when he was 13. Have faith!

149 Think you've got it rough? On days when it's hard to find anything to appreciate about your life, **think about how it was for girls in the not-so-long-ago past.** Just a tiny blip ago in history, women couldn't own homes or land or businesses. They couldn't work at all in most professions and they couldn't even vote to change things! The few women who were allowed to work earned far less money than men who did the same jobs. Girls your age were destined for one thing only: marriage, and even that was often arranged by their parents! At 14 or 15, a girl would be forced to marry the guy her parents picked for her and spend the rest of her life cleaning, sewing, cooking, and taking care of lots of babies. Being a mom and housewife can be wonderful, but aren't you glad you have CHOICES?

150 Makeup can be fun, but be sure to use it to enhance who you are—not to change or cover up who you are. If you're already wearing makeup, chances are decent that you're wearing more than looks good on you. Teenage girls usually make the mistake of thinking "more is better" when it comes to makeup, but the opposite is actually true.

A little makeup can help you to look your best and feel really confident. But if the makeup you're wearing changes the way you look so much that you wouldn't want people to see you *without* makeup, you're overdoing it!

151 Be aware that department store makeup is a huge rip-off! The stuff that costs $5 in the supermarket comes from the same factory vats as the stuff that costs $35 in the fancy department stores. When you spend the big bucks, you're paying for the company's advertising and packaging, not a superior product. So save your money and splurge on a pricey haircut—that's one beauty area where you do get what you pay for!

152 Take a hike! Want to vary your workout or go out on an adventurous outing with friends? Find a fun place to hike. Don't forget to bring some sunscreen and plenty of H_2O.

153 Get out of a rut by going international! You may not be in a position to grab your passport and head for the airport, so try the exotic fare at an ethnic restaurant. Browse through a specialty import store.

TRY THIS!

Hook yourself up with a pen pal or cyberpal from a foreign country. Log on to http://www.girlslife.com/cyber.html to get one.

Borrow a fashion statement from another heritage, or pick up a few key words in a foreign language. Anything that broadens your outlook on humanity helps keep your everyday probs in perspective.

154 Sibs can be the greatest, or they can be your biggest nightmare. It's easy to think that because you share parents and genes with someone, you might have a few things in common with that person. Often it just doesn't work out that way. You may not consider your brother or sister your friend, but try not to make him or her your enemy either. Even if you wish you were born with different ears or a different eye color, you've learned to make the best of what you've got. Sibs are just like that. You're born stuck with them and you can't change them. The best thing you can do is find ways to make your relationships with them as good as they can be. First of all, don't expect your brothers or sisters to be like you or think like you. Even if you are as different from them as night and day, try to accept them exactly as they are, just like you yourself want to be accepted for who you are. If you can muster up even a fraction of the effort you put into your friendships and direct it toward your siblings, you may see some big improvements! We're talking all kinds of sibs here—step-sibs, half-sibs, whatever. Being on good terms with them can really reduce your stress and improve your enjoyment of that place you live in, so it's worth making the first few moves. After all, these same sibs are still going to be a big part of your life 10, 20, even 30 years from now when you can't even remember the names of the friends you're currently hanging with!

155 As you grow, your need for sleep varies. Listen to your body! You'll probably go through periods where you feel great on just seven or eight hours a night, but during other periods you might need as much as ten hours of sleep just to function the next day. Sleep deprivation can cause you to lose your edge in school and sports and even give you a gloomier outlook on life. Getting the sleep you need is one of the simplest things you can do to keep feeling good, so take advantage of it. And if you don't get enough rest one night, take a nap the next day!

156 Hug! There is something absolutely mega-magical about the power of a simple hug. Don't save hugs for special times—give them out freely to your family and friends. Hugs make people feel great and they help you stay emotionally connected to all your loved ones.

157 Think about how often you say these two tiny words: "I can't." They seem harmless enough, but did you know that every time you say those words you are chipping away at your self-esteem? When you say, "I can't," you are telling yourself (and the whole world) that you are powerless. Usually, there is another way to word it that would be better for your self-respect. If you're talking about something that you don't know how to do, try saying, "I haven't tried in-line skating yet" instead of "I can't skate." And even if you are just trying to get out of hanging with a particular friend, you *can* be honest without being cruel. Don't say, "I can't go to the game with you Friday night." Of course you could if you really wanted to! Instead, say, "I've already made plans to go to the game with some other friends."

CATCH THE BUZZ!

1984 Olympic silver medalist Peter Carruthers says, "When you're at your limit and your goal seems impossible, a little more work, patience, and positive thinking may lead you to the satisfaction of achievement."

158 Do you ever fantasize about changing your hair color, getting a tattoo, or piercing yourself in some way that involves more than just a hole in each ear? Fantasize away, but promise yourself that you'll never actually make any big alterations to your body! Stuff like tattoos or unnecessary perforations are a major mistake, because what looks kinda cool today could look majorly geeky tomorrow. And even though hair dyes do grow out over time, they can take a painfully l—o—n—g time to grow out when the color isn't what you'd hoped it would be (which is what almost always happens). If you're set on shaking up your look, there are lots of ways to do it with clothes, hairstyles, and accessories that you can easily CHANGE when you decide you hate 'em.

If you just gotta be a rebel girrrl, mess around with hair mascaras. They come in shock-value shades like purple, cherry red, and blue, and they wash out when you're tired of being an attention-magnet. To get just a streak of crazy color, buy a clip-on color piece. You just clip them right above your ears and brush your own hair over them so that the wild hue peeks out of your do. You can get fake tattoos and all kinds of clip-on body rings, too.

159 You may have heard a lot about releasing your anger and negative emotions so that they don't build up inside you. But don't forget to release your joy, too! Some people think to be cool is to walk around vaguely unhappy all the time, as though they have all these dramatic problems and they're too important to take a moment to be silly or joyful. That's not cool—it's dumb. Learn to celebrate even the tiniest good things in your life and you'll be a happier, more fun-to-be-with, more ALIVE chica!

CATCH THE BUZZ!
Actress Shirley Jones (you know—Mom Partridge!) says, "Repress nothing, neither the sweet nor the bitter. Let it out!"

160 If your best friend starts giving you the cold shoulder and acting withdrawn, you owe it to her to figure out what's going on. **Ask her what the problem is.** She could be in a funk that has nothing to do with you. Maybe something has happened in her life that's making her angry or sad and she's taking those feelings out on you because you're the person she's most comfortable with. Try to get her to talk about her feelings. If she gets defensive and denies that there's anything bugging her, tell her you'll give her some space right now, but you'll be there if and when she needs you. If you suspect she's involved in something she can't handle on her own, you may want to share your concern with others who are close to her. Being a true friend sometimes means doing what's best for the friend you love, even if it makes her temporarily mad at you.

161 **Stop regretting stuff.** Regrets are a total waste of time. Instead of thinking, *If only I had done blah-blah-blah*, program yourself to think, *Next time I will do blah-blah-blah!*

162 Are you artistic? If you're nodding your head, great—go for it! But if your first instinct was an automatic "No way!" read on. Art is a mega-hip way to get in touch with what's going on inside you, and you don't have to have one whit of talent to take advantage of it. Most people steer clear of artistic endeavors because they think art is only for the especially creative or talented, but art can and should be enjoyed by everyone. Some forms of therapy even use art as an outlet for expressing all kinds of feelings the patients don't even know they have. **Get creating** and tune into the true you!

CATCH THE BUZZ!

Feminist Gloria Steinem says, "Give yourself an opportunity to discover your own imagery. Walk through an art store and see what attracts you: using a sketchbook and soft pencils, getting your hand in wet clay, smelling oil paints on real canvas, sloshing brushes ove watercolors, feeling finger paints, or scrawling with big crayons . . Whatever you end up creating will be as universal as a human han and as unique as your fingerprint. The more regularly you create, the more you will notice an image often repeated in varying ways That is your true self made visible."

163 **Lighten up!** The next time you feel problems weighing you down, see if you can find something in them to laugh about. We've all been taught to take our responsibilities seriously, but that doesn't mean we can't have fun with them. Laughing about your problems won't make them go away and it won't solve them, but it can take the weight off them so that you can solve them more joyfully.

TRY THIS!

Here's a goofy little trick from the book *Laughter Therapy* by Annette Goodheart. Think about a problem you're having—let's say it's a bad cold that's keeping you from going to a party. Pretend the problem is your right hand. Flatten your hand, keeping your fingers together, and put it up to your face with the palm just touching the tip of your nose. That's how you've been looking at the problem! You can barely see around the problem and you'd probably trip over stuff if you tried to walk this way—so how are you supposed to solve anything? Now say "Bad cold—tee-hee!" as you immediately pull your hand about a foot away from your nose. Did the silliness of the exercise make you laugh for real? Look at how much more vision you have when you pull the problem back a little. It's the same size hand and the same size problem, but when you pull it back you can see the bigger picture. When you begin to see the problem in a less serious way, you'll have a better chance of coming up with good solutions to it.

CATCH THE BUZZ!

Author Kurt Vonnegut, Jr., says, "Laughs are exactly as honorable as tears. Laughter and tears are both responses to frustration and exhaustion, to the futility of thinking and striving anymore. I myself prefer to laugh, since there is less cleaning up to do afterward—and since I can start thinking and striving again that much sooner."

164 Nothing is worse than fighting with one of your closest friends. It's the people who mean the most to us who can make us the most furious! **Whatever is causing the fight, put it in perspective.** Few things are worth losing a true friendship over. Before you start sticking pins in a voodoo doll that bears a striking resemblance to her, arrange to get together to talk it out. Let her have her say, get everything off *your* chest, and figure out what you both have to do to patch it up.

165 Do you feel like you spend a lot of time waiting? Waiting is wasting precious moments of your life! Try to **plan in advance for times when you'll be waiting for something**—like when you're getting a haircut or waiting to see a doc or dentist. Bring a great book along or bring notes from school so you can get a head start on studying for your next test.

TRY THIS!

If you're caught without anything to read, like when you're waiting in a long checkout line at a store, play little people-watching games with yourself to mak the most of the time. Practice your creativity by looking at the other people in line and making up little stories about them. Check out the women and girls for any fashion idea you might want to borrow. Or start up a conversation with the person next to you—you might even end up enjoying the wait! You'll drive yourself crazy if you just stand there thinking, *I can't believe this is taking so long!*—getting annoyed won't make the line go any faster. You might as well have some fun!

166 Are you up against something really tough? Adults are often guilty of trivializing the problems of young people, but **if you're suffering because of something major that is going on in your life, keep looking for help until you find it!** If your parents don't understand, talk to your school counselor, an aunt, a grandparent, someone at your place of worship, or even a friend's mom. Don't suffer alone. There ARE grown-ups who want to help you—you just have to find the right ones.

167 You watch and wait for some sign that your crush likes you back—and sometimes that sign never comes. Don't let an unreturned crush get you down! Half the time the guys girls pick for their crushes are guys they barely know anyway. Even if he had returned your crush, you might have discovered he wasn't right for you once you got to know him.

168 At some point you might find yourself crushing on a guy you're already good friends with. If he's not romantically interested in you, don't just write him off as a creep. Since you like him as a person, be thankful for his honesty and keep him on your list of friends. If he's special enough for you to really know him and have a crush on him, he must be a pretty great guy. Enjoy his friendship for now. Who knows how he'll feel in the future?

169 What about when *you're* the crush? It can be uncomfortable when you find out a guy likes you and your interest in him is ZILCH. Even if he isn't your Romeo, be gentle with him. Think about how you felt the last time your crush didn't return your feelings. Be honest with him, but try to let him down without squashing his pride.

Q & A

Question! This guy has a crush on me and he won't leave me alone. He follows me around school and majorly gives me the creeps. What should I do?

Answer! If this guy is really upsetting you and talking to him just isn't working, go to a teacher or your school counselor. Especially if you ever feel threatened or in any danger, tell someone in authority about the problem ASAP!

170 The next time you're feeling stressed to the max, hug your dog or cat! It's been proven that pets make people feel better. If you don't have one, borrow a friend or neighbor's dog. Spending some quiet, peaceful time with a sweet, gentle animal can really help to put your problems into perspective.

171 Time . . . maybe you've got too much of it on your hands, or maybe it's the one thing you never have enough of. How you spend your free time says a lot about you. Are you involved in any school clubs or organizations? Do you take art, music, dance, or voice lessons, or play on sports teams? What made you choose the activities you're involved in now? Lots of girls get hooked up with certain programs just because they're considered cool or because their friends are doing it. But you'll be happier and get more satisfaction out of your life if you choose activities that really speak to YOU. Look inside and find your true passions. If you start developing skills now in areas you really love, you could be laying the foundation for a dream career!

CATCH THE BUZZ!

American statesman Ben Franklin said, "The Constitution only guarantees the American people the right to pursue happiness. You have to catch it yourself."

172 Everywhere you look today there's some sort of message about sex. But the messages are never the same, and that can be scary and confusing. No matter what your friends or your boyfriend or the media says, sex is NEVER "no big deal." For teenage girls, it's a very, very big deal. It can mess up your life and be just as deadly as drugs or alcohol, so take it SERIOUSLY. Talk to an adult you trust and let her help you sort out the facts. Love yourself enough to take care of yourself. Make a commitment now that you can live by throughout your teenage years—the commitment to do what's best for YOU.

173 If you ever have to be out late at night, like if you're walking home from a dance or a friend's house, remember the old buddy system. If you can't walk with a group or at least one friend, call home for a ride.

174 Want to get a workout while learning a valuable skill? Take lessons in self-defense! Hopefully, you'll never have to use what you learn, but knowing how to defend yourself from danger can give you a powerful sense of confidence. Martial arts are super-popular and they offer some cool psychological benefits along with the physical training. Lots of girls love strutting their stuff with karate, tae kwon do, or even kickboxing! Some communities offer classes especially for girls and women that incorporate a number of self-defense techniques. But beware! Even after all your training, when you're feeling like a lethal weapon personified, STAY AWAY FROM DANGEROUS SITUATIONS! No one is invincible and all your good efforts will be wasted if they make you so cocky you endanger yourself.

175 What *is* a woman's role these days? Does anyone know anymore? In one sense, it's great that so many options are open to us, but in another sense, we're almost made to feel incompetent if we don't do EVERYTHING! The only way to stay sane is to tune in to your feelings and do the things that feel right to YOU. If your idea of a fun weekend involves experimenting with soup recipes or knitting your own bedspread, it doesn't mean you won't run your own company someday. Don't let a fear of being labeled "domestic" or "old-fashioned" stop you from enjoying an activity you like. In recent decades, anything resembling traditional "women's work" got a bad rap, but now stuff like cooking and sewing is being glorified again— just look at Martha Stewart!

176 Want to gain some bargaining power with your parents? **Offer to take total responsibility for the family pet.** Maybe you already pitch in, but taking Fido for a few walks a week is not the same as taking care of him completely. If you're the one who regularly feeds him, bathes him, and walks him (or changes the litter box if Fido is a kitty), you'll be building valuable skills in the art of commitment—the most important tool necessary for success in almost anything. And the next time you want your parents to trust you with a privilege, you can point out to them how completely responsible you've been with the four-legged family sweetie.

177 Do you ever wish you had more clothes? Maybe you have more outfits than you think you do. The next time you find yourself zoning out in front of a movie channel for a whole Sunday afternoon, get off your duff and **play dress-up** instead. (Remember how much fun it was when you were five?) Take everything out of your closet and look at each piece of clothing as though you've never seen it before. Now pretend you're a mannequin in a store window and try all your stuff on in NEW combinations. Sure, your purple striped shirt looks adorable with the overalls you ALWAYS wear it with, but it might look great tied at the waist with your gray skirt, too. You always wear the collar open, but what if you buttoned it all the way up and wore a funky pin at the neck? While you're at it, pull out some of the jewelry you haven't worn in a while. Try doing your hair a different way. A whole new you could emerge!

178 What are your *expectations*? When you wake up in the morning, do you **expect to have a great day** at school, or do you expect that one thing after another will go wrong? Do you have any idea how powerful your expectations are? When you picture things in your mind, you can actually cause them to happen in real life! It sounds hocus-pocus, but it's true. Our thoughts are the seeds for everything we do and everything that happens to us. That doesn't mean that everything you imagine will happen—but imagining it is the first step to making anything happen! There's a thing called *expectation fulfillment,* and what it means is that without even realizing it, you can cause your expectations to come true, whether they are good or bad. Here's an example: Say a new girl moves into your neighborhood and you think it would be cool if the two of you became buds. If you meet her *expecting* that she will feel the same way, she'll probably think that you're friendly and fun and she'll want to be friends with you. But if you're feeling bad about yourself and you meet her *expecting* that she won't like you, she'll probably get a feeling that you wouldn't be much fun to hang out with. She won't want to be your bud and your expectation will come true without you realizing that *you made it come true*. It takes practice, but you can control what you let your mind think. Don't let it dwell on things that you don't want to happen! Be a positive thinker and you will soon have a more positive life!

179 If you want to change it, SAY IT!

Here's a little trick that lots of grown-ups use to make changes in their lives: They say *affirmations*. To affirm anything means to say it in a positive way. Affirmations are just positive statements that you make to yourself, but they have mega-magical powers! Always say your affirmations as though the thing is happening now. If your goal is a killer report card, say, "I'm a straight-A

TRY THIS!

Most of us could use a little boost in our self-esteem, so say some self-lovin' affirmations every day. You can't go wrong with a simple statement like "I am a beautiful, smart, responsible girl and all good things are happening for me." Saying it even just once a day could change your life!

student," even if you're not one yet. Don't say, "Soon I will be a straight-A student." When you say it that way, you keep it in the future. You have to pretend the thing you want is already happening when you say your affirmations. Affirmations work even better when you look in a mirror and say them to your own face, looking deeply into your own eyes.

180 Depression—almost everyone feels it sometimes. But you have the power to pull yourself out of it! The secret is to **be your own best friend.** Pretend that your best friend (you!) is depressed and ask her the following questions: What are you feeling bad about? What do you need to feel better? How can I help you feel better? How can I help you be happy? Write down all the answers in your secret journal or on just any piece of

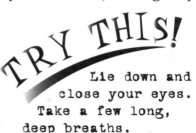

TRY THIS!

Lie down and close your eyes. Take a few long, deep breaths. Imagine your sadness as a color—whatever color comes to your mind first. Now imagine happiness as another color. Picture the happy color lapping against your body in gentle waves, slowly filling you up and washing away the sad color until you feel completely content.

paper. Do whatever you would do for a best friend who was feeling down—play soothing music, massage your temples, give yourself a big bear hug. Remember that sadness is a part of life, and see if there's anything you can learn from this particular depression. Then put it behind you and tell yourself it's time to feel better again. Close your eyes and imagine your inner joy bubbling up through the layer of sadness you've wrapped yourself in.

181 Are you a critical person? Do you say things like "I can't believe she's wearing those shoes" or "He's so stupid!" or "What a klutz!" or "That is the ugliest dress I've ever seen"? When you criticize others, you're actually making yourself look bad. By putting other people down, you're letting everyone know that you don't feel good about yourself. If you did, you wouldn't have to make yourself feel better at other people's expense. If you're critical of others, chances are you're critical of yourself as well. Do you ever think, "Why did I do that? I'm such an idiot"? You need to do whatever it takes to make you love yourself more! There are tips throughout this book that can help. Try to change your inner voice to a kind one and repeat positive affirmations about yourself. Say them every day and watch yourself change from a critical person to one who is accepting and loving toward yourself and others!

TRY THIS!

Say into a mirror, "I am perfectly lovable just the way I am," and "Everyone's doing the best they can, including me." Add any other affirmations that make you feel good.

CATCH THE BUZZ!

Educator Booker T. Washington said, "You can't hold a man down without staying down with him."

182. If that voice inside your head keeps nagging you with unhappy thoughts, try a thought-stopping trick. As soon as you realize you're having a negative thought, shout STOP! inside your head. Imagine yourself shouting it as loud as you can in your mind without actually making a sound. That should stop the gnarly demon-thought from taking over, and in time it could even prevent you from having negative thoughts in the first place. Say you're walking into the classroom where you're about to take a big test and the voice in your head is saying, "I should have studied harder. I'll never pass this . . ." Just mentally shout STOP! as soon as you

realize what you're doing. Then you can force your thoughts in a better direction, like "I'm going to know all the answers on the test. I'm smart and I've been paying attention in class and I studied a lot. I'm going to ace it." It's hard at first to even notice when negative thoughts are popping up, especially if you're used to having them all the time. But with practice, you can shout them right out of there before they cut you down.

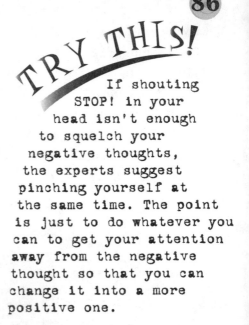

TRY THIS!

If shouting STOP! in your head isn't enough to squelch your negative thoughts, the experts suggest pinching yourself at the same time. The point is just to do whatever you can to get your attention away from the negative thought so that you can change it into a more positive one.

183 Stop whining—not only because your friends and parents are sick of hearing it, but because it's bad for your health! Did you know negative people get sick more than positive people? If you have legitimate complaints, by all means air them, but if you find yourself constantly whining about the same problems without ever taking steps to fix them, snap out of it! Instead of saying, "I wish blankety-blank would happen," say, "I know blankety-blank will happen," or "I'm going to make blankety-blank happen!" Then, if you try your hardest and the thing just doesn't happen, get past it! Focus on all the things in your life that ARE working.

CATCH THE BUZZ!

Our friend Jennifer told us this one: "There are two ways of looking at the holes in your shoes. You can dig the ventilation, or you can sing the blues."

184 Squeeze the area between your thumb and index finger the next time you've got a killer headache. Sounds weird, but some people swear by it!

185 What do you say when someone pays you a compliment? Lots of girls are embarrassed by compliments and don't accept them well. When a friend says, "Wow! You look totally hot today," your first impulse might be to say, "No way! My do won't swoop in the right direction and these pants make me look beastly." But just think about how nutso that is! You're telling the person who gave you the compliment that she is wrong or that she has no taste. If you do it often enough, people will stop complimenting you even when they're thinking nice thoughts about you. Try to think of compliments as unexpected little gifts. Always believe them and be grateful for them. The best way to respond is with a genuine smile and a simple "Thank you!" You don't have to talk about whatever they complimented, and you don't have to compliment them back right at that moment (that could sound fake).

186 If you like something about a person, pay a compliment. Personality compliments are appreciated even more than other kinds, so look for unique little things to compliment instead of just saying, "I like your shirt." If you see the school bully being especially creepy to a boy you don't know well, you could later say to the boy, "It was cool the way you handled Boris. He can be a mega-jerk, but you held your own without letting him get to you." That's the kind of specialized compliment that means the most to people. And it feels just as good to give real compliments as it does to get them!

187 Insults seem like the opposite of compliments, but they're really in a completely different category. Compliments are likely to be true, while insults are almost always just an expression of someone else's anger. Don't ever take an insult to heart. In fact, don't even let it ruffle one tiny little hair on your un-insultable head. When someone insults you, she is looking for a specific reaction from you. She'd love nothing more than to see you act hurt, surprised, angry, or defensive. And if you act in any of those ways, you can expect to be insulted by her again because you're giving her what she wants. No matter what the insulter actually says, remember that it's not really about you—she's the one with the problem.

When someone insults you, try your hardest to look like she hasn't upset you one bit. If a response is necessary, calmly ask her to repeat herself. Once she sees how cool and strong you are, she may back down and say, "Forget it." If she repeats the insult, just laugh and say, "Oh, that's what I thought you said," shaking your head as though she's the most ridiculous thing you've seen all day.

Question! Brittany is the most popular girl at my school and she really has it out for me. Every chance she gets, she embarrasses me in front of everyone. I don't know what I ever did to make her hate me so much! What should I do?

Answer! With a repeat offender, you need to change the pattern. Whatever you have been doing isn't working, so don't do the same thing again! Stay calm, stay in control, and simply ask her in front of everyone why she continues to insult you. Don't be whiny about it—just be curious. Your honesty will probably catch her off-guard. Say something like "Gee, Brittany, you really seem bothered by me. What is it about me that threatens you so much?" or "You must enjoy my company a lot more than I enjoy yours the way you keep coming over here to talk to me. The truth is, I just don't think you're much fun to be around, so why don't you stick to talking to your own friends and I'll stick with mine?" If you can pull it off without becoming the least bit emotional, she'll probably back down. If she doesn't, and she starts genuinely harassing you, tell a trusted teacher or adviser.

Q u i c k i e & A

188 If the person insulting you is a friend, you will have to do more than just laugh it off. Address the problem directly and immediately. You can't go wrong by honestly saying what you feel. Imagine one of your close girlfriends saying something to you like "You sounded so stupid talking to that guy." Instead of clicking into a state of despair over your miserable boy-skills, recognize her statement as an insult and remember that every insult is really about the person who makes it. Say to her, "It hurts my feelings when you insult me like that. Are you angry with me about something? Let's talk about it." If she won't admit that she's got a bug up her hiney, and especially if she insults you often, you may want to reevaluate this friendship. Say to her, "I like being around people who I can laugh with and enjoy things with. All you ever seem to want to do is bring me down. I don't want to hang with you anymore if you're going to keep insulting me." No matter what age they are, people always respect honesty. The more clearly you can spell out your feelings, the better your relationships will be.

CATCH THE BUZZ!

First Lady Eleanor Roosevelt said, "No one can make you feel inferior without your consent."

189 The natural look *is* the coolest look around, but that doesn't mean your face is a no-groom-zone! One glam way to make the most of what you've got is to do a careful brow exam. Do your eyebrows flatter your face and brighten your eyes in neat, curved arches, or are some strays running amuck? It may be tweezin' time! Perfect eyebrows are bona fide beautifiers, but don't go into this territory blindly! Weirdly plucked brows look, well . . . weird, and they take like a century to grow back. Here's a little pluckin' lesson: To discover the best shape for your brows, hold a pencil straight up against the side of your nostril so that it extends onto your forehead. Notice where the pencil meets your eyebrow.

That's where you want the brow to start. Now tilt the pencil across your cheek so that one end still touches the side of your nostril and the middle of the pencil is lined up with the outer corner of your eye. Notice where the pencil hits your brow—that's where it should end. Next, use a brow brush, fine-tooth comb, or old, dried-up mascara brush to brush your brows straight up toward your hairline. Look for strays—single eyebrows that are growing off on their own instead of sticking with the pack. Hold the pair of tweezers against your skin, close to the hair root, and gently grab ONE hair at a time. Hold tight and pull in the same direction that the hair is growing. (Pulling in the wrong direction could get you a red, chicken-skin lump!) After you've cleaned up the strays, see if your brow line needs any adjusting, but don't go overboard! Depending on the thickness of your brows, you may want to remove some hairs from the very bottom row to create a little more arch, but don't take out too many or you'll end up with a skinny little too-high line and that terminally surprised look.

TRY THIS!

If you hate pain (and who doesn't), numb up the area with a little ice or Oragel before the massacre begins!

190 If there's any other facial hair that's bugging you, don't pluck it, shave it, or wax it! You'll be sorry when it starts to grow back! Hit the pharmacy for some facial cream bleach. Jolen is the most pop brand; it comes in a little turquoise box. When puberty hits, lots of girls sprout a few dark hairs in that mustache area. Facial bleach is the best way to make them nearly invisible without causing the problem to worsen in the long run. Follow the package directions to the letter, and don't experiment with any bleach that isn't made especially for the face!

191 Got some extra time on your hands and want to learn a cool skill? **Go to the library and check out a book on American Sign Language.** It's not that hard to learn the basics— a lot easier than learning a foreign language! Learn it with your best bud, and the two of you will have your own secret code.

If you want to do something really worthwhile with your new ability to sign, volunteer at a local hospital, camp, or community center that has a program for deaf kids. It may take some time to find the right opportunity, but communicating with and making a difference in the life of a deaf child is an emotional experience you will cherish forever.

192 Real life got you stressed to the max? **Tune in to some toons.** That eternal cat-and-mouse chase may be just what you need to escape from your thoughts for a while.

193 Smoking is just plain revolting. It makes you smell foul, and it turns your teeth yellow and your skin gray. The coolest boys will not want to come near you if you smoke. A *Jump* mag survey found that 49 percent of guys said smoking makes a girl look insecure and 78 percent said they'd never date a girl who smokes. Maybe you know some kids who are already doing it. Even if they somehow manage to make it seem glam now, THEY WILL SOON REGRET IT BIG TIME. When you start smoking, you give away your power. You will want to stop and you won't be able to. You will spend all your money on cigarettes instead of all the other cool stuff you could be spending it on. You will get sick more frequently, causing you to miss out on parties and plans you love. No one

will ever want to hold your hand because your fingers will reek and your nails will turn yellow. When you're older, you'll pay more for auto insurance, you'll get nasty wrinkles at an early age, you'll have a harder time getting pregnant and having a healthy baby, and you'll increase your odds for osteoporosis (hunchback syndrome). Smokers are more likely to suffer from depression, get into fights, need therapy, and commit suicide. You have the facts! Don't be a stupid twit by doing something so unworthy of you!

Q & A Quick & Quickie

Question! My best friend swears that smoking cigarettes will help us to lose weight. Is that true?

Answer! Your best friend is way wrong. That's the final word from the experts. Kenneth Ward, PhD., is assistant professor of psychology at the University of Memphis, where they did a study to find out once and for all if cigarette smoking can help weight loss or prevent weight gain. The answer: NOPE! He says, "It's a big myth that cigarettes help control weight."

194 Join the fight against the ultra-losers who come up with all those slick cigarette ads aimed at YOU. Don't kid yourself—they know what they're doing. Are these money-hungry middle-aged suits your friends? Are they generously trying to introduce you to a product they think you might enjoy? GET REAL. These jerks know that cigarettes will hook you, make you miserable, and eventually kill you, but somehow it has remained legal for them to try their hardest to convince you how much fun it is to smoke. Their motives are crystal clear—YOU are paying their big, fat salaries with all the bucks you fork over to buy the nasty stuff. Maybe you think kids don't pay attention to those ads. Why, then, are the three most heavily advertised brands the same three brands that nearly all teen smokers buy? It's true and it stinks. The ads are designed to give you the idea that there's no catch, and lots of kids fall for it. But if you think you could smoke just a few cigarettes a week and not become addicted, you are dead wrong. That's exactly what 90 percent of adult nicotine addicts told themselves when they were your age. Everyone who starts thinks that she won't become addicted. No one says, "I think I'll be a chain smoker." But that's what happens. You become a slave for life and you look back and despise the day you struck that first match. It's time to get back at these cigarette company losers. Thousands of kids across the country are getting mega-riled at being slammed this way. For a free brochure on how you can join the fight, write to Campaign for Tobacco-Free Kids (Attn: Activity Guide), 1707 L Street, NW, Suite 800, Washington, DC 20036. For more info, log on to www.tobaccofreekids.org.

195 Getting on a plane? The air on airplanes can really dry out your skin, so be sure to bring some moisturizer and lip balm in your purse or carry-on.

196 Do you feel you have enough privacy? Private space can be hard to come by for a lot of girls. Maybe you have to share a room with a sis; maybe your parents feel your turf is their turf. Whatever the situation, you have a right to make your need for privacy known. Don't be surprised if your parents aren't supercool with it at first, though. Not too long ago, your life was pretty much their fishbowl. If you start deliberately hiding things from them or acting all secretive, they may suspect the worst. It's not that they don't trust you, it's just that they know that there is some way-bad stuff out there. The best thing you can do to earn the privacy you deserve is to have an honest conversation with your parents. Don't be afraid to bring up stuff that they may be afraid to bring up themselves. If you've been a trustworthy daughter so far, they'll probably be really relieved and impressed with your openness. Tell them

specifically how they can better respect your privacy. If you want more private time for phone chats with your friends, tell them how many hours per week you think is reasonable. If you want your closet and dresser to be off-limits to them, say so (but be prepared to do your own laundry!). If you want all visitors to knock before entering your room, put up a friendly reminder on your door.

Question! I have to share a room with my little sister and sometimes I want to kill her. How can I ever get any privacy with her around?

Q & A **Quickie**

Answer! Your sis would probably enjoy some privacy herself, so strike a deal with her. Pick a few hours on Monday when the room is yours and she has to beat it. Then on Tuesday, you scram while she gets solo-time. You and sis could alternate days or agree to a more flexible system, depending on your schedules. Coordinate visits from your friends to coincide with the hours that you have the room to yourself, and hang at their houses when it's your sister's turn. If the problem is that she's into your stuff, make up some firm, specific guidelines for what is and isn't off-limits to her. A nice, sisterly gesture might be to set aside one drawer where you keep a few things that she CAN borrow if she'd like. Let her know that any other drawer is a DO NOT ENTER zone.

197 Your bod is your bod and no one has a right to touch it in any way that makes you uncomfortable. **Don't ever, ever feel out of line in telling another person to take his or her hands off you.** If there's someone in your life who is touching you in a way that doesn't feel right to you, go right now to an adult you trust and tell her or him what's going on. Even if you promised you wouldn't. Even if you're afraid you'll make the person mad. Even if you think the touching might be your fault. IT'S NOT! If it sounds like we might be talking to you, don't wait another second. Put down the book, RIGHT NOW, and go tell someone about this problem.

198 Does the sound of your alarm clock jerk you out of dreamy-dreamy land with a nasty jolt? Do you feel like throwing the thing out the window? **Get one of those too-cool new gradual alarms!** Some feature a soft chime that starts out really slow and gradually gets more insistent until you're fully awake. Some have lightbulbs in them that slowly make your room brighter and brighter so you wake up as peacefully as you would if you were outdoors as the sun was rising. They can be pricey, so you may need to put in a request with Mom and Dad and wait for a gift-giving holiday. They are sooo worth it, though—you wake up feeling all mellow and lovey instead of starting the day with a panic attack.

199 PMS got you morphing into a meanie-monster? It's not uncommon for girls your age to wig out a little during that just-before-period time. But knowledge is power, so take advantage of the fact that you've wised up to the problem and **pull out all the stops to regain your peppy, life-lovin' attitude!** Meditate, do your visualizations, and get plenty of rest. In spite of the fact that you may be craving an entire chocolate sheet cake plus 45 Devil Dogs, it's especially important to eat well when you're PMSing. Remind yourself that bingeing only feels good while the food's in your mouth. After that you'll just feel full and gross and the carb overload will make your mood swings even worse! Research has proven that calcium helps reduce PMS symptoms, so make sure you're getting 1,300 milligrams a day.

TRY THIS!

If your calcium intake isn't up to snuff, try those yummy new chewy calcium supplements. They taste like chocolate candy—just what you feel like reaching for on those crank-demon days!

200. Dare to speak your mind! You're reading this book, so we know you're one ultracool chica. Don't be afraid to let everyone know it. If your gut feeling doesn't jive with what the crowd is doing, say so. Let everyone know exactly where you stand every time you feel your values are being put to the test. You may be afraid that some kids won't like you as much when they learn about your values system. You're right. Some won't. But who cares what losers like that think about you? For every kid who hears through the grapevine what you're all about and gets turned off, there will be another one who will get turned on. A LOT of girls and guys share your convictions, but they're not brave enough to talk about it. If you show them how to be proud of who they are, you'll have all the (truly) coolest kids in your school wanting to hang with you. And once it's common knowledge where you're coming from, you won't have to worry about some jerk trying to talk you into doing shots at a party. You won't have to worry about some undercover creep asking you out. You'll be respected for the outrageously hip chick that you are and you'll attract outrageously hip people to you. You have the courage to make it happen!